FRIENDS *of the*
Livingston Public Library

Gratefully Acknowledges
the Contribution of

Nancy E Cohen

For the 2017-2018 Membership Year

D0782274

BOUND TO THE FIRE

BOUND
TO THE FIRE

How Virginia's
Enslaved Cooks
Helped Invent
American Cuisine

KELLEY FANTO DEETZ

UNIVERSITY PRESS OF KENTUCKY

Scholarly publisher for the Commonwealth,
serving Bellarmine University, Berea College, Centre College of Kentucky,
Eastern Kentucky University, The Filson Historical Society, Georgetown
College, Kentucky Historical Society, Kentucky State University, Morehead
State University, Murray State University, Northern Kentucky University,
Transylvania University, University of Kentucky, University of Louisville,
and Western Kentucky University.
All rights reserved.

Editorial and Sales Offices: The University Press of Kentucky
663 South Limestone Street, Lexington, Kentucky 40508-4008
www.kentuckypress.com

Library of Congress Cataloging-in-Publication Data

Names: Deetz, Kelley Fanto, author.
Title: Bound to the fire : how Virginia's enslaved cooks helped invent
  American cuisine / Kelley Fanto Deetz.
Description: Lexington, Kentucky : The University Press of Kentucky, 2017. |
  Includes bibliographical references and index.
Identifiers: LCCN 2017029779| ISBN 9780813174730 (hardcover : acid-free
  paper) | ISBN 9780813174747 (PDF) | ISBN 9780813174754 (ePub)
Subjects: LCSH: Slaves—Virginia—Social life and customs. |
  Slaves—Virginia—Social conditions. | African American cooking—
History. | Cooking, American—History. | African Americans—Food—
Virginia—History. | African American cooks—Virginia—History. | African
American cooks—Virginia—Biography. | Slaves—Virginia—Biography. |
Plantation life—Virginia—History. | Virginia—Race relations—History.
Classification: LCC E445.V8 D44 2017 | DDC 641.59/296073—dc23
LC record available at https://lccn.loc.gov/2017029779

In loving and respectful memory of Jody Kelley Deetz,
VeVe Anastasia Clark, James Fanto Deetz,
and the ancestors

CONTENTS

Introduction: In Myth 1

1. In Home: Standing the Heat 15

2. In Labor: Cooking for the Big House 43

3. In Fame and Fear: Exceptional Cooks 73

4. In Dining: Black Food on White Plates 99

5. In Memory: Kitchen Ghosts 127

Acknowledgments 141

Notes 143

Bibliography 161

Index 173

IN MYTH

Cecily Hemphill wakes early on a Saturday to make her girls breakfast. Looking into her cabinets, she realizes she is out of pancake mix and runs down to the Safeway on Lakeshore Avenue in Oakland, California. Meanwhile, Jim Keller is in Sioux Falls, South Dakota, plotting his menu for tomorrow's Sunday brunch. He too heads to the local grocery to shop. In Boston, Shann Whynot-Young runs to the corner market to fetch some syrup for the family. Down in Tampa, Florida, Jennifer Hercules is staring at the syrups in the grocery aisle and reaches for a familiar and affordable choice. All four people choose Aunt Jemima to help them make a quick and reliable meal. Something about her smiling face ignites an instinctual response from consumers. What is it about this name, this face, and, specifically, the lure of the brand that causes people to buy this product? Is it simply the low price and the familiarity, or is it the four centuries of marketing black cooks as trustworthy kitchen help? Aunt Jemima is the iconic enslaved cook. But who does she represent, and what do we know about those who actually cooked for their oppressors?

In American popular culture, enslaved cooks have been either portrayed as Uncle Toms or romanticized by the popular image of Aunt Jemima.[1] As one of the most prevalent and lasting images of slavery, the black cook is found in everything from grocery ads to cartoons, and as a result, American consumers have become accustomed to this imagery. Having the picture of Rastus on a box of Cream of Wheat or Aunt Jemima pancake mix in your cupboard leads to an uninformed yet intimate familiarity with these icons. The idea of the nonfictional black cook has become ingrained in American domestic culture, sitting alongside canned goods on grocery shelves and at breakfast tables, without questioning the reality of their position in American history. Through systematic primary research, this book uncovers the centrality of the cooks' role both in the kitchen and in the larger plantation community. Who were these men and women who were forced to cook for those who enslaved them?

This book is an interdisciplinary study that focuses on eighteenth- and nineteenth-century enslaved plantation cooks in Virginia and explores the influence of their legacy on twentieth- and twenty-first-century American memory. To render their significance in American cultural and social history, this work draws on archaeological collections, cookbooks, plantation records, material culture, folklore, and cultural landscape studies.

Plantation cooks were highly skilled, trained, and professional. They created meals that made Virginia famous for its cuisine and hospitality, and they were at the core of Virginia's domesticity and culinary pride, as well as at the heart of the plantation community. Enslaved cooks existed between two worlds— living and laboring in their enslavers' homes, under their watchful eyes, yet belonging to the larger enslaved community who resided in field quarters away from the main house. These cooks occupied this liminal space and used this axis to manipulate their existence in the brutal culture of chattel slavery.

The legacy of enslaved cooks, or of house slaves generally, is riddled with myths rooted in misunderstandings of the past. Fictional sources such as the "Willie Lynch Letter," which illustrates a strict antagonistic division between light-skinned house slaves and dark-skinned field slaves, have created a hysteria of false proofs that feed the hunger for answers about the past and continue to mislead eager-minded folks to sources that are not, in fact, real. As a result, these enslaved domestics are depicted as docile, loyal slaves who had little connection to the larger enslaved population. This book unveils the richness of the archives and other sources related to those who worked inside plantation kitchens and offers a nuanced look at an aspect of history that gains as much from myth as it does from reality. It examines how we choose to remember the past, versus what the evidence suggests. This work engages in direct conversation with the folklore surrounding the loyal, happy house slave and presents a counternarrative to our historical imaginations.

The archaeological and historical records demonstrate the centrality of the cooks' role in the plantation community, and their material culture shows how these cooks created a black landscape within a white world and were able to share this unique space with the larger enslaved population. Their voices are often hidden in the recipes recorded in handwritten cookbooks, in the archaeological remnants of their material world, in oral histories, and in some documented slave narratives. Their labor constituted only a portion of their lives, while their cultural influence is firmly demonstrated by the retention of African foodways in American cuisine. Some of their personal stories provide compelling evidence of the complicated relationships that existed in the social world of southern plantations. Enslaved domestics used their skills to manipulate their enslavers. They were subversive and intentional and remained anchored to the larger enslaved community, despite their physical location within the big house.

The legacy of enslaved cooks is best seen in twentieth-century grocery advertisements, black Americana, and material culture.[2] The popular icon of Aunt Jemima, as well as other lesser known black cooks, reinforces consumers' racialized and gendered ideas of authenticity and food quality, while informing Americans' memory of enslaved cooks and their current place in our lives. These recognizable icons have been a staple of American culture, leading to a false familiarity with the idea of enslaved cooks. The marketing of these images has made them so familiar that we have neglected any rigorous investigation into their role in history. The overuse of this imagery invites a critical look into their real lives and begs for a better understanding of their experiences, their living and working conditions, and their actual legacy in American culture.[3]

In Virginia, the labor and expertise of plantation cooks became essential commodities, as they were critical to the success of domestic performance and the creation of Virginia's hospitable lifestyle.[4] This book brings forth the hidden voices of these enslaved plantation cooks and supplements existing studies on mistresses, enslaved communities, and domestic labor. Unlike studies of foodways, this book concentrates on the cooks themselves, rather than the food they produced. Other scholarship has unveiled the detailed evolution of African American foodways and their significance in American culinary history.[5] Enslaved African and African American cooks used traditional West African spices and ingredients in their dishes. Foods such as okra, peppers, and yams and dishes such as gumbo and fried fish were all part of the culinary knowledge they brought with them from their African homelands. These skills and tastes were handed down from generation to generation and significantly transformed American foodways.[6] This cultural retention and reproduction flourished within the slave quarters and accompanied the enslaved cooks into the main house, thus transforming elite dining preferences and southern cuisine as a whole. Although cuisine is an essential element of the enslaved cooks' legacy, this study focuses on uncovering their daily rituals, labor, family life, housing, and socialization to provide a dynamic interpretation of their struggles, pride, pain, sorrow, dignity, and joy.

There is still an overwhelming notion that the plantation mistresses were the ones who cooked all the food for their guests and families, when in fact their enslaved cooks performed this task. Scholarship, plantation tours, and popular rhetoric of the plantation table are rife with this myth. In part, this book is a response to Katharine E. Harbury's *Colonial Virginia's Cooking Dynasty*, which outlines Virginia's culinary past in incredible detail. However, Harbury fails to mention that enslaved cooks actually prepared all the food and that they were the reason for the existence of this "dynasty." Similarly, the mystification or, often, misrepresentation of the source of this labor does not escape the secondary literature, which has fueled this lie for over a century. *Bound to the Fire* places the enslaved cooks at the core of this "dynasty" by confronting the widely accepted idea that the mistresses produced Virginia's famous cuisine.

WHY COOKS?

I arrived at my decision to explore the lives of Virginia's enslaved cooks through multiple avenues. I spent my early years cooking in restaurants and in private homes. The labor was physically challenging and mentally trying. On the one hand, I was able to express my creativity through food. On the other hand, I was treated poorly by many folks, and I often hated my job. The environment changed, depending on where I worked and how much effort I put into the food. My pride was always at risk, and the labor took a toll on my body. In the end, these factors led me to leave the professional kitchen.

I have spent more than twenty years visiting and revisiting a series of Virginia plantation museums. The tours focus on the main house, lingering in the halls, parlors, and bedrooms and providing immense details about the white people who sat in the chairs, waited in the halls, and graced the plantation's landscape. Occasionally these tours include a brief pass through the kitchen and then continue on, as if nothing or nobody existed in that space. But the smell of old fires, the sight of decaying iron pots, and the thought of hard labor would overcome me every time, leading me to stay behind and try to envision that room in use. My historical imagination was ignited, fueled by vision and smell. This experience led to my quest for more knowledge. Unfortunately, the tour guides are typically uninformed and often deflect any questions about the enslaved population. As the years passed, I continued to revisit these plantations and ask questions about the kitchen folk. Some improvements have occurred in this regard at the larger plantations, but static interpretations remain at the smaller, less funded ones.

A thorough review of the literature on slavery led me to ask more questions about these cooks, whetting my appetite for more answers. These answers were absent in the sources available, but when I looked at the primary records, these cooks' stories started to appear. I found them hidden in the recipes in a mistress's handwritten cookbook, in archaeological field notes and archaeological deposits, and in the sights and smells of the cooks' living quarters above the kitchen, where they rested and spent time with family. As a former cook myself, I would like to be remembered for more than my food. My cooking techniques are important in understanding my culinary training and influences and how I spend my days, but I am more than a recipe. Similarly, enslaved cooks were more than the dishes they were forced to make, and this book unpacks the rest of their stories. It is by no means an exhaustive study of every enslaved cook and plantation kitchen in Virginia. It is, however, an attempt to render their stories and to situate them in a place of importance, with the hope that this will act as a building block for future studies.

Virginia is rich with history, filled with historical homes and kitchens that have remained untouched for centuries. These archaeological and architectural footprints tell the stories of those who passed through these spaces, and this study extracts the distinct voices of the enslaved cooks who contributed to Virginia's historical legacy but have gone unmentioned for far too long.

A BRIEF HISTORY OF VIRGINIA

The colony of Virginia was established in 1607 after King James I issued a charter authorizing the Virginia Company of London to settle somewhere in North America. On May 14, 1607, 104 English colonists arrived at Jamestown and established Britain's first successful colony in North America. Additional male settlers followed.

At this point, food was a function of living rather than any sort of explicit cultural expression. These early settlers ate what they could: rats and other vermin, grains, and even each other when necessary. By the winter of 1609, the lack of food resulted in more than 400 settlers dying of starvation.[7] In 1620 the Virginia Company sent 90 unmarried women to Jamestown, followed by more the next year. This attempt to balance the gender ratio signified a transition from a satellite settlement to a long-term colony. The creation of family life is recognized as the beginning of a white Virginian domestic space.[8] The early settlers, now accompanied by women and indentured servants, focused on building homes and farming tobacco. As the colony began to take shape, so did the labor market.

The influx of black labor into the Old Dominion began early. Virginia's black community is almost as old as the colony itself. The distinct Afro-Virginian experience began in 1619 when a Dutch ship dropped off "20. and odd Negroes" near Jamestown.[9] Their status as free or enslaved was not recorded, but their presence in Virginia marked the beginning of an African (and later African American) presence in the new English colony.[10] The seventeenth century was a turbulent time for the English settlers and laid the foundations for a plantation society. Early Virginia plantations were established along the James River to enable easy access to transportation and facilitate the movement of crops. These early plantations focused on tobacco production and relied on both indentured servants and enslaved Africans to plant, grow, process, and transport tobacco.[11] Kingsmill (established in 1619), Flowerdew Hundred (1619), and Shirley Plantation (1613) were some of Virginia's first tobacco plantations and were models of success and wealth in the eyes of the white settlers.

During this early period in American history, the South has been referred to as a "society with slaves" rather than a "slave society," reflecting the evolution of a racial caste system in America.[12] Toward the end of the seventeenth century, plantation owners exhibited a preference for enslaved Africans over indentured servants; the Africans' lifelong status as slaves and their superior agricultural skills made them more attractive than indentured whites with only seven-year contracts. While the first generation of Afro-Virginians was likely indentured, the follwing generations were undoubtedly enslaved. In 1625 there were only 23 Africans in Virginia; by the middle of the century, there were as many as 300. By 1640, some Africans had been bound to a life sentence of servitude. In 1661 Virginia statutes known as the Slave Codes formalized the legality of and preference for enslaved labor. These laws applied not only to adults but also to their children, who were born into lifelong enslavement.[13] By 1705, Virginia passed a series of laws that governed the actions and status of enslaved blacks and solidified a race-based caste system of slavery.[14] It was during this period that the early plantations were constructed, Virginia's domestic realm was created, and the role of enslaved cooks took shape.

During the late seventeenth century, the Royal African Company was responsible for enslaving and shipping 1,000 recently captured Africans to Virginia every year. By 1708, there were 12,000 Afro-Virginians and 18,000 whites; by 1756, the Afro-Virginian population had grown to 120,156, compared with 173,316 white Virginians.[15] In 1790 there were 292,627 enslaved blacks in Virginia, or roughly 39 percent of the total population. Thirty years later in 1820, the slave population had almost doubled, with 206,879 enslaved women and 218,274 enslaved men; 80 percent of the enslaved population lived on rural plantations. By 1860, there were 241,382 enslaved women and 249,483 enslaved men. On the eve of the Civil War, the vast majority of the 4,308 plantations housed between 20 and 40 enslaved people, and 1,355 plantations had 40 to 100 enslaved people working and living on them. There were 113 plantations in Virginia that housed between 100 and 300 enslaved folks; these large plantations were most likely to have a designated enslaved cook who performed specialized tasks.[16]

By the early eighteenth century, more than half of Virginia's African population consisted of Igbo from Nigeria. As the century progressed, more enslaved Africans were brought from the Bight of Biafra and Angola, and by 1739, they made up 85 percent of the newly enslaved.[17] These ethnic affiliations are important in understanding the skills of Virginia's enslaved Africans, especially their knowledge of foodways, medicines, and poisons. Although Igbo were preferred as field hands, there is no doubt that, given their high population percentage, many of them cooked in the main house.[18]

The vast majority of enslaved folks were put to work on plantations. Tobacco was Virginia's main crop until the eighteenth century. Because growing tobacco depletes the soil's nutrients, many planters diversified their cash crops to replenish the soil and maintain a steady or increasing income. Alternative crops such as corn and wheat were planted, and the latter became a predominant crop by the end of the eighteenth century. By 1850, the once booming tobacco plantations in the Piedmont region of Virginia were producing significantly more wheat than tobacco, and on plantations with more than twenty-one enslaved people, they were producing more than twice as much wheat as tobacco. However, unlike tobacco, wheat's growing cycle required only short bursts of labor and did not constantly occupy the enslaved labor force. Thus, during the nineteenth century, many enslaved folks were sold south through the domestic slave trade, as well as hired out as skilled laborers.[19]

Plantation society took on many characteristics over the three centuries of its existence. Seventeenth-century plantations were small, and the planter often worked alongside indentured servants, enslaved Africans, and African Americans. White women labored in the field too, and they also cooked, cleaned, and cared for the domestic space. By the late seventeenth and early eighteenth centuries, changing ideas about race and class began to transform plantation culture. The increase in tobacco profits caused an influx of Englishmen who hoped to benefit from Virginia's wealth, and who brought with them an elite cultural standard.

With this influence, a new patriarchal plantation culture formed, with the planter as head of the household. This resulted in a gentry that was somewhat disconnected from the direct management of enslaved laborers. Plantation owners hired overseers—often poor whites or the sons of planters—to manage, control, and punish the enslaved. The planters' wives remained in charge of the domestic sphere and coordinated formal functions such as dinner parties, balls, and dances, but they no longer labored alongside the enslaved. [20] This lavish lifestyle enjoyed by elite white Virginians was possible only because of their heavy reliance on skilled enslaved laborers. Enslaved Afro-Virginians functioned as blacksmiths, brick masons, farmers, laundresses, butchers, seamstresses, and cooks on these large plantations, and it was their forced labor that allowed Virginia's plantation culture, and ultimately the nation, to thrive.

Enslaved laborers who worked in the fields typically lived in the field quarters, and those who worked as domestics resided in close proximity to the main house. Sometimes neighboring plantations were close enough for the enslaved populations to interact with each other, and they often took advantage of the footpaths connecting nearby homes to maintain a sense of community. By the middle of the eighteenth century, race and status were melded, and a caste system was firmly in place. Enslaved people now had to be issued passes by the overseer in order to travel off a plantation. This made visiting neighbors' plantations stressful, cumbersome, and, most important, illegal.[21] Even so, a rich, vibrant African American community developed within the confines of enslavement and influenced many aspects of American culture. Many scholars have studied this phenomenon, although less attention has been paid to the culture of those who lived and worked within the planters' homes.[22]

BREADTH, SCOPE, AND LIMITATIONS OF THIS BOOK

This study is both a social and a cultural history, and it shows how the cooks' expression and manipulation of food reflected larger cultural transmissions throughout the African diaspora. This work focuses on the people who labored in Virginia's plantation homes, specifically those large enough to have a designated cook. On smaller plantations (generally those with fewer than twenty enslaved people), the cook also served as the laundress or the maid, and the stories of these individuals differed from the stories of those who worked solely as cooks on large plantations. Enslaved cooks were sold as such, and they often worked in grand homes. This study explores their experiences to represent what life was like on big plantations, where the kitchen was separate and the cook fulfilled the highly specified role of producing food for the big house.

Locating the cooks' voice in the historical records was a challenging task that was fruitful at times and empty at others. At the start of my research, I cast a wide net that included the records I already knew existed. The eighteenth-century *Virginia Gazette* is ripe with data on enslaved cooks, as are the nineteenth-century slave narratives. As a result, I limited my research to the eighteenth and nineteenth centuries, including Virginia as it was before the Civil War, along with what is now West Virginia. As my archival search continued, the richest material came from the Tidewater region, the Richmond vicinity, and the Piedmont area.

Defining a neat chronological narrative arch proved almost impossible. The thinness of the early records forced me to rely more on material culture, and the richness of the later sources led to other problematic issues. Additionally, the slowness of technological advances in the kitchen sphere muddled many of the experiences together. Open-hearth cooking was the standard, and kitchens like the ones seen at Poplar Forest and Monticello were rare. Similarly, the recipes were handed down generation to generation, and although techniques were surely improved over the years, this was rarely noted. My approach to using recipes as a lens into labor yielded valuable insights, but it was not without error.

Presumptions were sometimes made. For example, well-known published cookbooks offered insights into recipes that proved successful, but I assumed that a recipe published in 1860 had been around for decades before making its way into a cookbook.

Much of Virginia's recorded history was burned during the Civil War, leaving historians with what survived the fires and whatever records remain in repositories. Even when written records are rich, they typically take the white perspective and rarely discuss the lives of the enslaved with any sort of intention or objectivity. The art of narrative building is challenging when dealing with the African American past. Fortunately, archaeology and landscape studies help fill the gaps of the written record, but they still pose problems when trying to avoid generalizations, and interpretations are always somewhat subjective. This work is my attempt at extraditing some of the voices of those who were silenced through law and oppression, and I consider this stewardship an honor and undertake it with complete humility.

History is like a mosaic in which defined individual experiences make up larger sweeping narratives. Any approach to understanding the past leaves room for criticism and neglect. However, understanding that pictures can be painted in many ways and with several layers means that every addition brings us closer to the past. It is my hope that this work captures some of the individual voices while providing enough generalizations to illustrate the larger picture that resonates in our collective memories. Overall, this book seeks to redefine how we remember, acknowledge, and promote the legacies of enslaved cooks, and it grants them full cultural authorship of southern foodways.

The five chapters create a multiangled perspective based on different elements of the cooks' lives. Chapter 1, "In Home," introduces the cooks through the physical spaces—the kitchens—in which they worked and lived. Starting with the most obvious evidence of their lives, these kitchens provide a stage to imagine the social and cultural history examined in the remaining chapters. Chapter 2, "In Labor," illustrates the daily lives of enslaved cooks, highlighting their routines, their struggles, and their unique world. Resistance went hand in hand with oppression, and their labor was a tool that allowed them to gain moments of power. Chapter 3, "In Fame and Fear," offers several cameos of individuals who rose to fame through their roles as enslaved cooks. Some of these cooks were known for their culinary skills, others for their acts of poisoning their enslavers. These men and women were well known by Virginia's plantation elite, and their reputations caused either panic or envy among the slaveholding population. Chapter 4, "In Dining," puts both African food and enslaved cooks at the core of white Virginians' culinary pride. It also dissects the very intimate relationships between the white family's needs and the labor of the enslaved. Chapter 5, "In Memory," draws the attention from the past to the present and challenges public sites to be more responsible with their interpretations of the past. If the past is everything that happened before now, and if history is how we choose to remember it, how will we "remember" these cooks? It is my hope that this book is a first step toward asking more questions, and eventually finding more answers, about the men and women who were bound to the fire.

One

IN HOME

Standing the Heat

SURRY COUNTY, VIRGINIA, 1860

It was the eve of the Civil War, and Sookey went to bed every night thinking about the labor of her days. Cooking on a Surry County plantation was a stressful task that occupied all of her five senses and consumed almost every moment of her life. She provided several meals a day to the white family who enslaved her and to whomever came to visit. Food was more than sustenance; it was at the core of Virginia hospitality. Her friends in the field worked from sunup to sundown, while Sookey remained bound to the fire in the big house's kitchen twenty-four hours a day. She was forced to cook multiple meals that were both scheduled and spontaneous. Up every day before dawn, Sookey baked bread for the mornings, cooked soups for the afternoons, and prepared divine feasts for the evenings. She roasted meats, made jellies and puddings, and created desserts for every free person who passed through the plantation.

Sookey lived in the kitchen; she slept upstairs above the hearth during the winters and often moved outside come summertime. Her children learned to cook and work in the big house and were always under the watchful eye of the white family. Private moments were rare, as was the ability to truly rest. She rose early to bake, cooked all day, and went to bed with the next day's menu both in her mind and on the large hearth on the first floor of her kitchen quarters. Cooking for a Virginia plantation was a challenging task, one that required culinary talents, nuanced social skills, and physical strength. The labor was intense—lifting huge pots of water, standing for hours by the open fire. Her workday bled into the night, with no space for respite. Sookey was a typical enslaved cook and undoubtedly worked herself to death. Cooking provided her and her family with a unique status within the bonds of enslavement, but it came at a high price. In 1860 Sookey died at age fifty from a hemorrhaged womb, likely caused by overexerting herself for the sake of Virginia's famous hospitality.

Sookey was born near the banks of the James River sometime around 1810, two years after the United States withdrew from the transatlantic slave trade. She was about twenty years old when Nat Turner organized and executed his revolt in nearby Southampton County and transformed the culture of slavery. Fear, abuse, and control plagued Virginia's plantation communities. Sookey was central to one of the most turbulent eras in American history. Her role as a cook subjected her to the direct gaze of white Virginians at a time when enslaved folks were increasingly involved in plotting insurrections and poisoning their enslavers. The black body represented strength, anger, and a complex dependency. Part of this dependency rested firmly on Virginia's dining room tables. Southern hospitality relied almost exclusively on enslaved domestic labor. Sookey was burdened with an incredible responsibility, as her skills solidified the reputation of her enslavers and that of Virginia as a whole. Guests wrote countless missives about the meals they ate while visiting Virginia, often attributing the food to the mistress of the house. Although these white women may have helped design the menus or provided some of the recipes, it was the enslaved cooks who created the meals that made Virginia famous for its culinary fare.

CHARLES CITY COUNTY, VIRGINIA, 2016

Grand plantations pepper the landscape along Virginia's Route 5. To drive through rural Virginia is to gaze back into the nineteenth century; it is visually striking and has remained mostly untouched over the past 150-plus years. The homes of Virginia's elite white families have held up over time, while the slave quarters have been demolished or allowed to fall back into the earth. The more you know about the history of these buildings, the more it hurts when you see slave quarters destroyed. These buildings are direct reminders of the people who called them home. Their walls speak volumes across generations, and they remind us that the ancestors persevered. They are like tombstones marking the lives of millions of enslaved Africans throughout the diaspora, and when they stand tall, they invite questions about and inspire answers to one of the darkest moments in history. Their vanishing only reinforces the idea that such places do not matter and that these homes—symbols of pain and survival—are unworthy of preservation, memory, and respect. These buildings are where enslaved folks created families against incredible odds, and they are essential parts of the American story.

Plantation kitchens, though built with slightly better materials than the average slave quarters, are also reminders of those who dwelled inside. Once you see these architectural skeletons, they are impossible to unsee. To perceive a landscape as a window into the past is to welcome an understanding of both the history of slavery and its legacies. The built environment is our connection to the past, and the surviving kitchen quarters are invaluable resources in understanding Virginia's enslaved plantation cooks.

The Plantation Kitchen

By the end of the seventeenth century, Virginia was experiencing a critical ideological shift. The concept of race, a social construct to explain physical differences and promote white supremacy, began to take root. The influx of indentured servants, juxtaposed with a growing reliance on enslaved African labor, directly influenced Virginia's vernacular architecture. Plantations transformed rapidly, reflecting emerging and changing views on race. This shift is clearly visible in the evolution of kitchens within the larger cultural landscape. Between the seventeenth and nineteenth centuries, Virginia's plantation kitchens mirrored the greater social environment and the position of enslaved cooks within the larger plantation community. By the turn of the twentieth century, the legacy of this racialized space was transferred directly into modern kitchen spaces, and it continues to inform our collective memory of cooks and their roles in society.

People build things that make sense to them, and such structures represent the builders' ideological perspectives. Architectural historian Dell Upton considers "landscape as [an] extension of ideological process."[1] This view enables a critical evaluation of space and place as markers of social customs, mores, and materializations of cognitive patterns. Therefore, examining kitchens within the larger context of plantation landscapes uncovers the centrality of this designated space in Virginia's plantation culture. Why were kitchens built the way they were, and how did they change over time? How did this transition reflect ideas about race and place, and how did it ultimately affect the enslaved cooks who lived and worked inside these buildings? To understand the people who occupied these buildings, we must start with the physical world they lived in.

Virginia, like many of England's colonies, was a microcosm of Britain. However, its individuality was seasoned by local environments, resulting in a distinctly Virginian tradition. In the early seventeenth century Virginia planters owned relatively small dwellings, compared with their typical eighteenth-century mansion-style homes. "These were one-and-a-half-story frame structures with one or more rooms on each floor."[2] The kitchen consisted of a hearth in the common room, and it was part of the shared social space of the household. Vernacular house forms in Virginia began as varieties of English house plans. By the end of the seventeenth century, they had become explicitly Virginian and housed common folk as well as elites.[3] This distinctly Virginian house was based on a combination of the colonists' need to culturally reproduce English architecture and the local frontier needs of the Virginia landscape.

With the increased reliance on enslaved Africans and indentured servants, Virginia planters began to evaluate the social strata. "Increasingly in the period 1660–80, planters moved servants and slaves to separate buildings, creating a definite spatial division where no clear social one existed, and built smaller houses for themselves."[4] A major ideological turning point came in 1676, when Bacon's Rebellion—an attempt by poor whites and enslaved Africans to overthrow the local government—influenced elite planters to reevaluate the class-based social strata.[5] As a result, Virginia's elite began the strategic ideological promotion of white supremacy. This divide-and-conquer technique succeeded in breaking the burgeoning rebellious spirit and, in turn, transformed a class-based society into a racially conscious Virginia where blacks were enslaved. By the late seventeenth century, the planters' choice of small houses and outbuildings for servants and slaves reflected the growing social separation between master and servant.[6]

This increasing racial consciousness was transferred to the

cultural landscape as planters began to divide spaces into distinct categories. The idea of "otherness" informed the architectural plans of Virginia's plantations. "Elite whites, carefully orchestrated exercise in the definitions of space, delineating two spaces: white and black/poor white."[7] The most significant example was the advent of the external kitchen. "They also built a separate kitchen, a separate house for the Christian slaves, one for the negro slaves."[8] "The addition of new rooms reflected an analytical desire for order and separation that grew out of and amplified the seventeenth-century division of servant and served spaces."[9]

This division of space was noted in 1705 by Robert Beverly, who stated: "All their drudgeries of Cookery, washing, daries, etc., are perform'd in Offices detached from their Dwelling-Houses, which by this means are kept more cool and sweet."[10] Plantation museums rely on this quotation to explain the phenomenon of kitchens being erected outside of the main house. It is a sterile way of justifying white Virginians' decision, after a turbulent quarter century, to erect separate buildings to house enslaved cooks and the equipment they needed to furnish food for white families. It is no more than a mythical romanticizing of the past to think that, in an era when bathing was infrequent and there were fireplaces in every room, removing the kitchen would improve the smell of the home and reduce the fire risk. It simply does not add up. Plantation kitchens, which began inside the common space of the typical two-room house, were moved to external locations to physically separate the servants from the served, creating a mental template that defined otherness.[11]

THE EXTERNAL KITCHEN

"Separating the kitchen from the main plantation house was one of several related architectural gestures that signaled the onset of a more rigid form of chattel slavery that would persist until the middle of the nineteenth century."[12] Seventeenth-century Virginian planters continued to live in rather small dwellings, while their servants moved into separate domiciles. "In the early eighteenth century, small houses of this general character served even the wealthiest segments of the population."[13] Hall and parlor houses became increasingly popular, and within twenty-five years, most of Virginia's elite had adopted the house form known as the Georgian-style house.

This architectural transformation paralleled Virginia's evolving social traditions. Builders adapted to the planters' desire for compartmentalized spaces and for a particular flow throughout their homes.[14] At the turn of the eighteenth century, and with the racial caste system in place, Virginians began to upgrade their material style. At this point, British domestic buildings were undeniably influenced by architectural greats such as Vingboons, Palladio, and Serlio. Virginians, however, had a hand in creating their own culturally specific architectural formation, a combination of local and extralocal influences on the Georgian style.[15] In the 1930s scholar Dixon Wector interviewed Marian Cater of Shirley Plantation, who told him that the kitchen was separate from the house "since no matter what the hazard of cold dishes, the gentry of Virginia believed that cooking had no business under the same roof as eating."[16] This is a break from the typical public narrative, which cited the risk of fire as the cause for architectural separation. As cooking was performed by black people, and formal eating was done by whites, this sort of language speaks to the social reasons for an external kitchen and the importance of racialized spaces in the presentation of food.

By the early eighteenth century, elite whites in Virginia organized their society around values of patriarchy, localism, and hierarchy.[17] The popular Georgian style of architecture fit with this ideological perspective. Named for the English kings George I through George IV, who reigned between 1714 and 1830, this style was popular in Virginia until around 1780. It was characterized by rectangular symmetry and was stylistically inspired by Classical, Renaissance, and Baroque forms. Another characteristic of Georgian houses was the formal central hall, which acted as a public space, separating the adjacent semiprivate and private rooms from company.[18] This physical layout established distinct spaces that reflected rigid social roles, and it allowed the physical compartmentalization of race, class, and gender within the architectural form.

This Georgian house form developed alongside and in response to changing views about race and servitude. The compartmentalization of space reflected the ideological shift toward the Georgian mind-set that permeated the construction of eighteenth-century plantation landscapes.[19] Georgian house plans were ideal for separating social spaces and creating a controlled flow throughout the rooms. This architectural style undoubtedly functioned to support the needs of the Virginia planter class.

During the early eighteenth century, white America and England maintained a certain level of political and social consensus.[20] Virginia planters looked toward England as the cultural motherland and tried to re-create the Georgian way of life. The Georgian mind-set was particularly evident in the performance of rituals of hospitality.[21] Planters presented their homes as venues for entertaining, and as such, they adapted their homes to produce a particular level of hospitality. Upton argues that "local builders took new ideas into consideration but were not overwhelmed by them. In eighteenth-century eastern Virginia, builders systematically dismembered the new architectural concepts and fit them into traditional Virginia ones in ways that illustrate the close interdependence of local and extra local impulses in vernacular building."[22] This local impulse included the centrality of kitchens and dining rooms for proper entertaining. Virginia's plantation homes assumed a unique shape that differed from homes in England and even in New England, where the kitchen remained inside the main house. With these transitions, elite women and enslaved Africans played critical roles in the functions of the plantation home.

A Culture of Hospitality

External kitchens provided a space to delineate race and class, and as such, they provided a place to nurture the roles of enslaved domestics in relation to the functions of the plantation elite. The Georgian mind-set directly influenced the emergence of the formal kitchen, and the formal or external kitchen preceded the development of dining rooms and halls. This order signifies a transformation into a culture of hospitality, where entertaining was part of the planters' projected image and drove mistresses' sense of domestic pride. "Eighteenth-century [social] planning was a painstaking operation that involved the careful correlation of space and social function."[23] The changing social habits of Virginia's elite planters led to the desire for more space than that offered by the traditional two-room house.[24] Planters thus called for the physical and ideological division of public versus private space and the construction of specialized rooms. The building of formal kitchens and ballrooms and banquet halls reflected the centrality of the culture of hospitality, and such places were essential to its functioning.

In contrast to the seventeenth century, when the vast majority of white Virginians were men, the eighteenth century brought more white women to the colony. With this shift came a drive for entertainment, and by the eighteenth century, it was a critical part of plantation culture. The rise in large-scale plantations created a sense of isolation that was assuaged by local socialization. "The large planter set himself at the center of a private community that replicated in form and appearance the civic order of public service."[25] Neighboring plantations became a community, as each took turns hosting dinners and balls. The kitchen became a distinct place to perform the ideological customs manifested in producing food, catering, and entertaining.

The rise in hospitality within these microcommunities called for increased attention to culinary fare. Virginia was now an established colony, and it needed to perform as such. English elites were used to fine cuisine, and as Britain's cultural child, Virginia needed to respond accordingly. Whereas food had been seen as merely a necessity for survival in the seventeenth century, there was now an increased desire to produce noteworthy meals as part of the entertaining platform. This, in turn, made kitchens, ballrooms, and enslaved cooks a higher commodity, as they were at the center of food production. The cooks' performance in the kitchen helped Virginia gain a reputation throughout the colonies for its hospitable nature.

The Manifestation of Wealth

Virginia plantations varied in size, function, order, and location. The larger the plantation, the more specialized its roles and buildings. For example, Shirley Plantation in Charles City County had a large external kitchen and a separate external laundry. Shirley was one of Virginia's most prominent plantations, and as a result, the cook had his or her own dwelling, separate from that of the laundress. On smaller plantations, the kitchen tended to be combined with the laundry, and the enslaved domestics shared a living space. The grander the property, the more formal the service buildings. With large plantations being erected throughout the Virginia countryside, planters needed to make sure their homes functioned according to their cultural ideologies, including notions of status, race, and gender. "Virginians also looked for neatness and order in their social lives. Their houses were part of a complex landscape defining and vitalizing that order, and changes in interior spaces can only be understood in the context of that whole landscape."[26]

Planters organized their land to display their wealth and control their space, which was "designed to indicate the centrality of the planters and to keep them aloof from any visitors behind a series of physical barriers that simultaneously functioned as social buffers."[27] Plantations were set up to exude an air of wealth. The main house usually sat on the highest point of the land, with the kitchen close by, usually adjacent to the dining or hall area of the main house.[28] This sort of spatial arrangement reiterated and reflected the social hierarchies of the planter and the enslaved folks who lived on the plantation.[29]

The main house had its own set of formalities, with public, semipublic, and private spaces. "The semipublic nature of the planter's house is evident, as is the extent to which he viewed it as an emblem of himself and his order."[30] The heart of the planter's order was his hall, which acted as the nucleus of his world. It was the center of entertaining and of public displays of wealth. The hall was the meeting point between the inside and outside worlds. It was in this space that planters performed and mimicked an Anglo-inspired elitism, putting on balls, dinners, and other social gatherings. The construction of halls increased significantly by the second quarter of the eighteenth century, providing a formal stage for entertainment and socialization. But the cook, laboring in the private space of the kitchen, was kept away from the front stage, thus promoting a sense of the mistress's accomplishments, while hiding the real star of the kitchen within the confines of the highly compartmentalized Georgian house style.

The transformation from a two-room house to a multiroom mansion allowed the creation of formal public space as well as private space. These designated rooms were divided along gender lines, giving the man of the house the formal stage of the parlor, dining room, and library. These divided spaces allowed a certain level of heterosocial interaction; however, the man had full and unconditional reign of every room.[31] By the middle of the eighteenth century, formal dining rooms were standard.[32] Georgian house plans suggested ways to incorporate these new spaces into traditional homes and how to control interior circulation—an architectural response to specific social requirements.[33]

In addition, room names changed significantly by the eighteenth century. Seventeenth- and eighteenth-century Virginians created a system of social categories—habitual ways of grouping and classifying particular daily activities and personal relations that underlay the physical layout of their houses. These bourgeoning classifications became room names that crystallized the intersection of physical spaces and social categories in a single term.[34] For example, an examination of probate inventories reveals that the architectural terms *passage* and *dining room* arose and were commonly used by the end of the first quarter of the eighteenth century and continued to grow thereafter.[35] By the mid-eighteenth century, plantation homes had a formal hall—a public room without access to other parts of the house—as well as a dining room, which was a semipublic space and often had an exterior door facing the kitchen outbuilding.[36] These rooms were highly masculine in their use, yet the dining room, as a semipublic room, acted as liminal space between the mistress and the cook, as well as between the planter and the public.

In contrast, the kitchen was the heart of the mistress's order—a feminine managed place. The naming system allowed the materialization of social custom into house plans.[37] The kitchen and the cook were the mistress's responsibility, and she was driven by the productivity of domestic ideals. During the nineteenth century, plantation mistresses were occupied by domestic performance and the desire to gain entrance to the elite world. This drove them to aspire to a particular level of cultural production in terms of food and entertainment. Thus, the kitchen became an essential part of the cultural landscape. The vast majority of eighteenth-century real estate advertisements listed the kitchen directly after the main house, indicating its status as the second most important building on a plantation.[38] Dimensions of the main house and the kitchen were listed, while the other dependencies were simply stated, without details. When Gabriel Penn listed his 274-acre plantation for sale, he stated that the property had "two kitchens, one of which is very valuable."[39] This advertising tactic speaks to the centrality and importance of a properly working kitchen as a selling point among Virginia's potential plantation owners.

A Feminized Landscape

The most exceptional example of a landscape designed for the sole purpose of entertaining can be seen at Stratford Hall Plantation in Westmoreland County, the birthplace of Robert E. Lee. The rise of entertaining influenced the design and function of many plantation homes, but none compares with the Lee property. Built in 1738, this home is rumored to have been designed by the mistress herself—Hannah Harrison Ludwell, wife of Thomas Lee. In any case, her influence is inarguable. Her son Charles Carter Lee wrote in disdain, "See what it is to be ruled by a woman. I should [not] have been now living in a house like this . . . had not my father been persuaded by his wife to put up this very inferior dwelling now over my head."[40]

Unlike traditional hall-and-parlor homes, this early Georgian-style house has a colossal entertainment hall at the core of the building, with entries and exits on each side. The entire southwest quadrant of the 9,000-square-foot home was built as a support wing for entertainment. This quadrant has two wine cellars, a winter kitchen, several servants' quarters, a massive storeroom, and, on the main floor, a large holding room for the staging of food before it was served in the adjacent dining room. Mrs. Lee's influence is unquestionably evident in the architectural proportions, which express her belief in the centrality of entertainment. Of the home's total 9,000 square feet, 3,600 are dedicated to specialized black labor.

THE KITCHEN QUARTERS AS HOME AND WORKPLACE

Most enslaved plantation cooks lived in the external kitchens, where their living conditions differed vastly from those of the folks who worked in the field. Although slave quarters varied in size and quality, a common eighteenth-century field cabin was one story tall; it had an external entrance and two main rooms separated by a central chimney. In the nineteenth century this pattern evolved to add a doorway connecting the two internal rooms. One of the two rooms had a loft to maximize occupancy, housing anywhere from six to twenty-four people. The average single dwelling measured twelve by eight feet; larger ones, in the style of dormitories, might be as big as sixteen by twenty feet and were split up into individual domiciles.[41] The slave quarters were part of two intersecting landscapes: the black landscape existed within and around the field quarters, while the white landscape surrounded the main house. From the masters' perspective, the slave quarters were part of the "working landscape," dictated to some degree by their location.[42]

Field quarters were of similar construction as poor white housing. However, poor white Virginians tended to live within the walls of their homes and with far fewer people. Here, "living" refers to the use of a designated space for eating, cooking, and so forth.[43] In contrast, slave dwellings were only a segment of the living space, and they were occupied by significantly more people. The enslaved population expanded its domestic space beyond the walls of the cabins and into the yard. This yard acted as a functioning work space, but it was mostly a social space for enslaved folks to conjure, eat, and maintain a sense of community. Slave quarters were constructed to facilitate this socialization and to allow for the ample development of surroundings.[44] This space also served as a way for the overseer to keep an eye on the slave community, proving a sense of panoptic fear among slaves. Enslaved blacks often built fences or buildings in an attempt to obscure the overseer's line of sight and combat this sense of surveillance.[45] Although these small garden fences did not completely obstruct the overseer's view, they provided a slight visual block.

In contrast to the field quarters, kitchen quarters reflected a microcosm of the big house. "Private" space was provided in the upstairs sleeping quarters found in most external plantation kitchens. This clear division of work and home space was unique to enslaved cooks and their families. Kitchens were the most common outbuilding listed in the eighteenth-century *Virginia Gazette*, with a total of 334 mentions, and they were the most clearly described. Even though kitchens varied in size, their layout was more standardized than that of other dwellings, most of them being two-room structures ranging from 192 to 384 square feet.[46]

The domestic slaves lived and worked within the white landscape. Many of them slept in a room inside the mansion, but the cook's living space depended on the location of the kitchen. Although most large-scale Virginia plantations had constructed external kitchens by the eighteenth century, some kept their internal kitchens and continued to house the cooks within the main house in a room adjacent to the kitchen.[47] This was a departure from the detached kitchen arrangement that prevailed in eighteenth-century Tidewater Virginia. This internal kitchen was one of four general styles of kitchen that enslaved cooks lived and worked in during the eighteenth and nineteenth centuries (the other three were external and are discussed below).

Mansions were not abundant in eighteenth-century Virginia; there were approximately two dozen by 1776.[48] Most eighteenth-century main houses had a hall, parlor, chamber, and/or dining room on the first floor. By 1750, the dining room, hall, chamber, and passage were the most essential public rooms, while the kitchen was the most important private space for domestic production. The presence of the dining room as a distinct social space filled with etiquette, props, and elite social functions became standard by 1750.[49] Naming a room was a way to acknowledge its social significance; however, the lack of a name speaks to the importance of "negative space" within the walls of Virginia's homes. In discussing the Moore House in York County, Upton notes the lack of a name for the back "fourth room." In a sense, the fourth first-story room was an "unwanted" space. Probate documents show a variety of contents, including "domestic items" and "Negro clothes."[50] There was no set name for this room, and it had no social meaning to the planters.[51] The absence of a proper name is significant. Because of the room's proximity to the internal kitchen or the dining room, it could easily be associated with enslaved cooks or domestics. This unlabeled space speaks to the invisibility of enslaved domestics, who existed to create a sense of

Figure 1. Kitchen at Stratford Hall. (Theodor Horydczak [circa 1890–1971] Collection, Library of Congress)

sophistication and attain elite domestic ideals, but in the shadow of the proud mistress and from behind the hidden passageways of the plantation.

The more common external kitchen usually sat adjacent to the main house, sometimes as part of a row or street that was visible from the main house. Its exterior resembled the main house in style but differed in construction.[52] These external kitchens generally came in three forms. The first was a small one-room cabin with a variously sized chimney (see figures 1–4). The chimneys depicted in figures 1–3 encompass an entire wall of the quarters. This type of structure was most likely used as both a kitchen and a laundry, given the width of the hearth and the adjacent fireplaces. The sleeping quarters would be in a loft opposite the fireplace.

The building depicted in figure 4 was a combination kitchen and weaving room; the kitchen was on the first floor, and the weaving room was located upstairs, presumably within the cook-weaver's sleeping area.

The second type of external kitchen was a two-room dwelling with a central chimney.[53] The fireplace was either along the back of the dwelling or in the middle of the kitchen space, dividing the internal space in two. If the chimney was along the back wall of the kitchen, there would commonly be a ladder or stairs along the internal side wall leading to a loft above. If the fireplace sat as a divider between the two halves, the space could be split in multiple ways. Similarly, the third type of external kitchen had fireplaces on the gable ends of the kitchen (see table 1).

THE KITCHEN AND DINING ROOM AS PLACES OF POWER

The kitchen, though separate from the mansion, was placed so that the windows faced the main house. It can be assumed that this allowed the mistress to watch over the cook, or at least it bolstered the notion that her eyes were on the kitchen at all times. The

Table 1. Layout of Two-Room External Kitchens

Location of Fireplace	First Room	Second Room	Second Floor
Central chimney	Kitchen	Living	—
Central chimney	Kitchen	Laundry	Loft
Central chimney	Kitchen	Scullery	Loft
Gable end chimney	Kitchen	Laundry	Loft or second floor
Gable end chimney	Kitchen	Scullery	Loft or second floor
Gable end chimney	Kitchen	Kitchen	Loft or second floor

Figure 2. Summer kitchen at Custis-Lee Mansion. (Theodor Horydczak [circa 1890–1971] Collection, Library of Congress)

main door was usually placed toward the dining area, to promote the flow of service from kitchen to table. The placement of the windows and doors encouraged a constant association between the main house and the kitchen and between the mistress and the cook. By the beginning of the nineteenth century, architectural trends transformed this virtual connection into constructed spaces. Enclosed colonnades, hidden walkways, all-weather passageways, and "whistling walks" (see chapter 5) were built as a response to many factors. Whereas the seventeenth century defined the separation of enslaved spaces and the eighteenth century formalized this partitioning into highly structured working landscapes, by the nineteenth century, the vast majority of kitchens were external, and plantation homes were highly functional producers of domestic entertainment. Balls and banquets became synonymous with Virginian culture and hospitality.[54]

By the early nineteenth century, many Virginia plantations were adding colonnades, or all-weather passageways, between the kitchen and the main house. During the 1800s this colonnade between the dining room and the kitchen was enclosed, creating the "little house."[55] Late-eighteenth-century planters incorporated passageways inside the main house to cure the "problem of circulation."[56] But the external version of this "flow fixer" has a more complicated history than that suggested by contemporary plantation narratives. According to official tours at Berkeley, Monticello, and Mount Vernon, these covered walkways were built so that the enslaved cooks would not have to walk through rain and snow. Although this pragmatic explanation is true, the construction of these passageways coincided with a changing ideological perspective toward enslavement and public displays of wealth and servitude. Attaching a service wing to the main house became popular in the early nineteenth century, and some rural plantations created covered walkways and passageways from the dining room to the external kitchen.[57] Aesthetics can explain some of the popularity of these additions, but their true function—to conceal the daily activities of slavery—became more apparent as time went on.

Mrs. Eliza Bruce, the mistress of Berry Hill Plantation in Halifax, Virginia, installed a series of bells in the servants' rooms, each with a different tone for the person requiring a servant's assistance.[58] Discretion and efficiency ruled the architectural developments of Virginia's plantations. Berry Hill was designed in the nineteenth century and reflected the ideological desire to conceal and control the flow of enslaved bodies within the mansion's private space. This desire stemmed from a growing need to conceal the private and complicated interracial relationships within the

Figure 3. Keswick kitchen, State Route 711, vicinity of Huguenot, Powhatan County, VA. (Historic American Buildings Survey, Library of Congress)

plantation household during a time when slavery was subjected to intense international scrutiny.[59]

With the end of the transatlantic slave trade in 1808, planters were forced to reevaluate their position on enslaved servitude and labor.[60] The trend of constructing all-weather passageways began just as slavery was becoming a more significant part of the international dialogue. Debates over the morality of slavery plagued many Virginia planters, and the more high-profile the planter, the more likely he was to build a walkway between his kitchen and mansion. Entertaining guests from other regions or nations where slavery had been abolished forced these white slaveholders to create a flexible landscape that could hide their moral sins from disapproving guests. Presumably, these guests knew where they were visiting and that enslaved people would be present. However, these walkways provided an architectural distraction from the starkness of exploited labor.

These passageways also allowed the planter to control circulation to every room in the house.[61] White anxiety about slave revolts was rampant in the nineteenth century. In 1801 the attempted revolution in Richmond by enslaved blacksmith Gabriel Prosser sent shock waves through Virginia. White fear of black revolution weighed heavily on the minds of those who continued to enslave African Americans on their plantations. By 1831, when Nat Turner led his revolt against the planter class in Southampton County, Virginia, that fear had already solidified and manifested itself in the architectural design of domestic spaces. Enslaved domestics (waiters, cooks, and butlers) were partitioned off in ways that both hid them from whites' gaze and attempted to control their movements. Paranoia surrounding potential revolts, as well as possible social "cross-contamination" from black liberators, caused these physical spaces to become more constrained.

While it is clear that the work of enslaved cooks and domestics differed from that of other laborers, they had the additional burden of being in the public eye.[62] They were part of the display of wealth, sophistication, and order of the domestic space. This was especially true at the larger, more prestigious plantations, where enslaved cooks created extraordinary meals, enslaved waiters served them, and white planters and their guests enjoyed every aspect. But what happened when their guests did not support a slaveholding ideology?

In addition to walkways, black servitude was hidden by other means. The perfect example occurred at Thomas Jefferson's Monticello. After his travels to Paris, Jefferson decided to re-create a system of high-tech dumbwaiters so that food and wine magically appeared out of the walls in the formal dining room. He also relied on a tiered table that could be set with one course on each tier, enabling a waiter-less dinner. His house was equipped with the most modern and bizarre gadgets to allow the presentation of food without blackness. His all-weather passageway, dumbwaiters, and hidden doors all shielded his guests from the black presence. Jefferson's Monticello is an extreme example of this attempt to hide black domestic labor, but it was nonetheless a marker of the nineteenth-century ideological shift toward a more racialized, self-reflective planter society.

Dumbwaiters served at the intersections of race, power, performance, and reputation beyond their functional role. They masked the black body in the semipublic space of the dining room. This was the essence of the dumbwaiter's popularity, and it demonstrates the social and political currency surrounding the dinner table. Domestics had been trained to perform at formal social affairs, and they were fully capable of being quiet during a meal. Having a piece of furniture sitting adjacent to the table, holding all the food, was not a simple replacement for a butler or a waiter. How was it easier for the guests to serve themselves in a culture that relied on servitude? This phenomenon could easily be associated with the rise of nineteenth-century abolitionist literature, or it might simply reflect the social unease that came with the closing of the transatlantic slave trade to the Americas or the increase in slave revolts. Moreover, there was a growing fear that the political discourse surrounding abolition or discussions related to black revolutionaries would be heard by the enslaved domestic staff and ignite revolutionary action on their part.

The Materiality of Plantation Kitchens

Plantation kitchens were fully furnished to conduct work as efficiently as possible. Kitchens had comparatively more furnishings than other outbuildings, and they were undoubtedly better equipped than the cabins in the field quarters. Kitchens were

Figure 4. Westover kitchen building, State Route 633, Charles City, VA. (Historic American Buildings Survey, Library of Congress)

unique, in that they had all the available amenities, but given the cooks' enslaved status, their access to such amenities was limited. Living and working in the big house allowed enslaved cooks to witness material wealth, but they owned little themselves.

Most external kitchens resembled the main house in both style and material. The majority of tiles were made of brick, and the floors were usually plain compressed clay, brick, or oyster shell rather than wooden planks. Whitewash was often applied to the interior of the kitchen to promote a "finished" or visually clean look. Kitchens were usually proportionate to the mansion; they were larger than most other outbuildings and sat adjacent to the main house, near the kitchen garden.[63]

The interior varied as much as, if not more than, the exterior.

The furnishings changed drastically between the late seventeenth and nineteenth centuries. Whereas seventeenth-century cooking technology consisted of an iron pot over an open flame, the eighteenth century brought the common use of Dutch ovens, salamanders, and more sophisticated tools. With the invention of the stove in the mid-1800s, the material culture of kitchens became increasingly technical. What had been reserved for the governor's palace during the eighteenth century made its way into plantation kitchens. These elite kitchens were stocked with fat skimmers, fish forks, trivets, mortars, stew stoves, and countless other elaborate tools.[64]

Although kitchen furnishings varied, most of them had the basic necessities. Along with the obvious hearth cooking area, some had formal dressers for rolling bread and baked goods. These dressers also provided storage for plates, pots, pans, and utensils. In her 1836 *Cooks Complete Guide*, Esther Copley argued for the importance of these furnishings: "Kitchens should be furnished with a dresser, over which a clean cloth should be kept spread."[65] This indicates the importance of presenting the kitchen as a "visually clean space" and suggests that the mistress was responsible for maintaining this particular ideal. The presence of a scullery in a room adjacent to the kitchen helped keep the latter visually clean. Many sculleries had "slop drains" for washing food items, dishes, pots, and so forth. These sculleries facilitated the flow of the kitchen by separating the business of cleaning from the production of food.

Much of the food, especially butter, sugar, liquor, and other valuable ingredients, was kept locked up in the main house.[66] This lock-and-key system intensified during the nineteenth century as mistresses became paranoid about the possibility of revolts and the overall cognitive dissonance among the enslaved population. They worried that cooks and field hands would steal these items for their personal consumption, thus taking away the mistresses' sense of control.[67] The temptation to take food items must have been overwhelming for cooks, as they had to smell and taste these products on a regular basis.

As mentioned earlier, cooks usually slept above the kitchen, either in a loft or on the second story. Their beds varied in size and quality, ranging from a basic straw mat and a wool blanket to a framed flax mattress. The cook's kin was typically allowed to live in this area as well, without having to share it with others. This was drastically different from the field quarters and even the domestic dormitories, where the sleeping arrangements sometimes ignored familial and biological bonds.

Although this could be viewed as beneficial for the cook, the reality was far from ideal. The field hands may have had to bunk alongside twenty-five other people, but they did not have to sleep next to a burning fire. The field hands often cooked in the yard, especially during hot days and nights. In contrast, the cook had to use the hearth regardless of the weather. This consistent use of the kitchen as a workplace interfered with the cook's comfort in his or her living and sleeping quarters. Tutor Phillip V. Fithian recalled that the cook often slept outdoors to keep cool.[68]

Just as field laborers found innovative ways to make their cabins "home," enslaved cooks did the same. They carved pictures into the walls of the second floor and persevered for the sake of their families and themselves. At Shirley Plantation in Charles City County, the kitchen has been restored as part of the plantation tour. Since the plantation has been in the same family since its inception, many of the original fixtures remain, as well as the utensils, pots, pans, and the like. The most significant artifact is a set of iron candleholders in the shape of Sankofa, an Akan symbol signifying the importance of looking back to move forward, retrieving from the past to look ahead, or, literally, "go back and fetch." Their placement in the kitchen workplace is a reminder that the cooks were as connected to their roots as the field hands were. Even though they were housed away from the rich cultural space of the field cabins and yards, they remembered their roots and displayed such icons within the white landscape of the plantation.[69]

These kitchens stand tall next to the mansion homes of Virginia. Their stories are rich, and their presence is a direct reminder of a culture that benefited from exploited black labor and the creative talents of enslaved cooks and established a lasting international reputation for southern hospitality. These buildings were home to hundreds of enslaved cooks and their families, and they used these spaces to carve out little moments of joy. Sookey spent her life working and living in a plantation kitchen, and her experiences were shared by countless others. To survive enslavement and maintain dignity in sorrow is a testament to the resilience of these people, and the built environment should be a lasting testament to their stories. These kitchens are standing monuments to those who labored within their walls. They beg the question of who lived in these kitchens, and how did they use their physical and social positions to survive slavery?

Two

IN LABOR

Cooking for the Big House

Before sunrise on a hot summer day in 1767, Sukey Hamilton, the governor's cook, began melting butter for the day's meals. This task, while seemingly simple, required constant attention and a delicate hand. Hamilton had likely been taught the following technique:

> Nothing is more simple than this process, and nothing so generally done badly. Keep a quart tin sauce-pan, with a cover to it, exclusively for this purpose; weigh one quarter of a pound of good butter; rub into it two tea-spoonfuls of flour; when well mixed put it in the sauce-pan with one table-spoonful of water, and a little salt; cover it, and set the sauce-pan in a larger one of boiling water; shake it constantly till completely melted, and beginning to boil. If the pan containing the butter be set on coals, it will oil the butter and spoil it. This quantity is sufficient for one sauce-boat. A great variety of delicious sauces can be made, by adding different herbs to melted butter, all of which are excellent to eat with fish, poultry or boiled butchers' meat. To begin with parsley—wash a large bunch very clean, pick the leaves from the stems carefully, boil them ten

minutes in salt and water, drain them perfectly dry, mince them exceedingly fine, and stir them in the butter when it begins to melt. When herbs are added to butter, you must put two spoonfuls of water instead of one. Chervil, young fennel, burnet, tarragon, and cress, or peppergrass, may all be used, and must be prepared in the same manner as the parsley.[1]

Hamilton not only had to constantly shake the pan but also had to keep the temperature and consistency of the roux at the perfect levels. Melting butter, a seemingly simple task, required skill, strength, and perseverance. If the small gravy boat filled with butter took this much attention, what kind of labor went into the rest of the meal?

A network of enslaved folks contributed to putting food on the table. Inside the big house there were butlers, bakers, butchers, maids, scullions, waiters, and assistant cooks who made up this large "catering network." The cooks were at the core of this culinary team, and its members worked seamlessly to provide the most sophisticated dining experience of the time. The kitchen acted as a back stage (separate from the public front stage of the main house), providing a space for the cook and the mistress to negotiate their relationship behind closed doors. Plantation cooks were kept on tight schedules, performing their duties at precise times and with strict deadlines. Their skills were multifold, and their role was central to the plantation and to the larger enslaved community.

This culinary team produced both quality and quantity. Eighteenth-century tutor Phillip V. Fithian commented on the latter during his long stay at Robert Carter's Nomini Hall Plantation: "Mrs. Carter informed me last evening that this family one year with another consumes 27000 Lbs of pork; and 20 beeves.

550 bushels of wheat. Besides corn—4 hogsheads of rum, and 150 gallons of brandy." He observed the production of food on a large scale: "I walked, to the mill together with Mr. and Mrs. Carter; Miss Prissy and Nancy, to see them make biscuits and pack flour . . . here too I had a forfeit for kneading biscuits . . . the ovens bake 100 lbs of flour at a heating, they are in the bake-house two ovens."[2] Fithian's comments highlight not only the scale of food production but also the relationship between the field hands and the domestics. The web of enslaved labor was vastly interdependent, and each ingredient stemmed from another person's forced labor. Wheat was grown, harvested, and milled by enslaved farmers to provide flour for the cook to use in the kitchen. Brandy was made from fruit grown and harvested by slaves and then fermented by the enslaved cook. Rum came from the Caribbean, starting as sugarcane planted, grown, cut, and distilled by enslaved hands. Feasting in Virginia meant consuming the labor of slaves, literally eating the fruits of their labor. To dine at an elite plantation during the antebellum and late colonial periods meant that one was, without question, intimately involved with slavery.

Living in the Kitchen Quarters

Enslaved cooks both lived and worked in the kitchen, providing no separation between labor and rest. Typically, enslaved field laborers managed to carve out separate spheres for home and work. But plantation kitchens placed cooks in a liminal space—between white and black, enslaved and free, work and rest. Yet these kitchen quarters provided a distinct living environment for the cook and his or her family. Compared with field quarters, where twenty or more people slept in a one- or two-room cabin, the cook's quarters were larger, made from better materials, and shared only with his or her biological family. Although this living arrangement might be appealing to some, it came with added responsibilities and stress, as living within the white landscape meant twenty-four-hour monitoring by the white family and little privacy.

The benefits were often outweighed by the temperatures in the kitchen, which could exceed normal physical tolerances. There is no doubt that the kitchen was comfortable in the winter, as the large hearth kept the entire building warm. However, Virginia's summertime temperatures often rise above 80 degrees, and the 90 percent humidity pushes the heat index well over 90 degrees. Thus, the hearth fire burning at over 1,000 degrees would make the kitchen torturous in the summer months. As a result, enslaved cooks often slept outside in the summer, away from the heat but subjected to mosquitoes, horseflies, spiders, and snakes. One's sense of home becomes more abstract when the physical walls are a less reliable marker of place.

Living in kitchen quarters was an intense sensory experience. Added to the heat were the smells, which were often ripe. The romantic plantation dinner table filled with French-inspired delicacies was a far cry from the kitchen scene. That physical space hosted the butchering of meat, the cleaning of fish, and the cooking methods of a pre–germ theory kitchen. For example, to make headcheese, an animal head had to sit in a vat of lye-based liquid for more than a week. The cook would stir the pot daily, remove excess mold and growth from the head, and skim the top of the liquid. Headcheese—essentially a jellied loaf of head meat— was a delicacy and signified culinary refinement and high class. It graced the tables of the wealthiest planters and undoubtedly filled their kitchens with a pungent smell. Foaming vats of fermenting meat, drying blood, fish guts, and rotting vegetables were commonplace.

Kitchens were busy places that were set up for large-scale

catering. They were furnished with an abundance of utensils and had detailed inventories. The colonial era began with simple equipment, open-hearth cooking, and English-inspired foodways. This changed as kitchens and food became more central to the Virginia elite. By the early nineteenth century, kitchen furnishings were a measure of one's wealth. This particular inventory was noted in 1879:

> [A kitchen] must have a good stove or range . . . a kitchen safe, a bread block in the corner, furnished with a heavy iron beater; trays, sifters (with iron rims), steamers, colanders, a porcelain preserving kettle, perforated skimmers and spoons, ladles, long-handed iron forks and spoons, sharp knives and skewers, graters, egg beaters, extra bread pans, dippers and tins of every kind, iron molds for egg bread and muffins, wash pans, tea towels, hand towels, plates, knives and spoons for use of the servants, a pepper box, salt box and dredge box (filled), a match safe, and last, but not least, a clock.[3]

Probate inventories and plantation recipes reveal the diversity of equipment and their uses. The "essential objects found in eighteenth century kitchens [included] skimmers, Dutch ovens, salamanders, bellows, fish forks, ladles, toasting forks, grid irons, trivets, chairs, table, mortars, tea and coffee service."[4] Toward the end of the eighteenth century, the introduction of iron stoves transformed plantation kitchens, shifting the base of labor from the floor of the hearth to the stove top.[5] This was a slight improvement, but one that only the wealthy could afford. Enslaved cooks had to adapt to all these changes.

Some of Virginia's kitchens were joint laundries; others had sculleries set up for cleaning the kitchen's hardware. One writer advised: "Always keep your cook well supplied with soap, washing mops and coarse linen rags. I have noticed that if you give them the latter, servants are not so apt to throw them away. Insist on having each utensil cleaned immediately after being used. Once a week have the kitchen and every article in it thoroughly cleaned."[6] They cleaned the pots and pans with sand and used well water to rinse them.[7] A scullery maid or a relative of the cook typically performed this task. Sophisticated drainage systems were carved into the exterior grounds to flush the waste away from the kitchen; however, the lingering smell of dishwater, rotting food, and ash remained within the kitchen complex.

MATERIAL CULTURE

The archaeological evidence from a nineteenth-century plantation kitchen in Prince George County, Virginia, reveals some of the personal items of enslaved cooks. The kitchen at Flowerdew Hundred Plantation contained significant laundering artifacts, including pins, thimbles, buttons, and buckles. These items presumably fell off the clothes being washed by a woman named Keziah Jones, a domestic slave on the plantation. Jones's son Emmanuel was the plantation cook. The presence of buttons, buckles, and pins confirms the architectural record, because having two hearths usually indicated a combination kitchen-laundry site. However, these small items had multiple uses during enslavement. For example, buttons were often worn as pendants; similarly, buckles and thimbles made their way onto enslaved bodies as jewelry. Reusing discarded or "lost" objects allowed enslaved folks to reinterpret these forgotten items and create adornment for themselves as well as for friends and relatives in the field quarters.[8]

The metal artifacts—everything from cast-iron pots to delicate copper rings—also tell a story. The size and weight of these pots remind us of the strength it took to move such vessels when they were filled with food. Cast iron was the best material for hearthside cooking, and the cast-iron pot was the main appliance in the kitchen. It was used to cook everything from stews to mulled wine. Dutch ovens and skillets shared the kitchen space, but the cast-iron pot was the queen of the hearth.

Training

Many of Virginia's enslaved cooks were formally trained on the plantation, either by the mistress or by the head cook. Plantation papers reveal the system whereby cooks were trained and promoted within the kitchen hierarchy. In 1858 Dr. Richard Eppes's cooks, forty-five-year-old Susan and seventy-two-year-old Harriet, ran the kitchen.[9] Records reveal that by 1859, field hand Ursula Sanders had been recruited as assistant cook and was tipped 50 cents for good coffee on top of her $1 Christmas present. Susan and Harriet, the head cooks, received $5 Christmas gifts, which was second only to that of the butler, Madison Ruffin, who was given $10. By 1860, Ursula was still apprenticing under Susan and Harriet and received her $1 bonus for Christmas.[10] This record shows not only the hierarchy within the kitchen but also the fact that cooks were chosen from among the plantation's entire slave community. Although the cook's family members lived within the kitchen's walls, they were not necessarily next in line to inherit the position of head cook.

Some enslaved cooks were taught how to read as a pragmatic way to deal with recipes and food production. Mistresses may have spent time in the kitchen teaching their cooks the particularities of certain European dishes, but they also expected a level of autonomy from them. It is unlikely that the mistress stayed in the kitchen and walked the cook through every step. Instead, the cooks would either memorize the recipes or read them as they worked. The currency of proper food was so important that the teaching of basic reading became essential to guarantee culinary delight. It can be presumed that this skill was valuable to the larger enslaved community as well, for they could rely on the cook to read and write for those who could not. In addition to reading, enslaved cooks learned basic math. Counting, fractions, and arithmetic proportions are all essential aspects of cooking, and knowing how to double or triple a recipe was mandatory for large-scale plantation cooking. Precise measurement is especially imperative in baking to ensure that breads rise, biscuits bake, and cakes form.

FOOD PREPARATION AND TECHNIQUES

With multiple meals being prepared on both short- and long-term schedules, the kitchen was an active space. Plantation recipes reveal the breadth of items that occupied the kitchen and the cook's mind simultaneously. For example, if the day's menu consisted of morning biscuits, eggs, smoked meats, and jams; midday breads, roasted meats, and soups; and evening game, stews, vegetables, and desserts, the cook would prepare some items that day as well as others, such as breads, jams, wines, headcheeses, and sausages, for later functions. Thus, cooks strategically scheduled their days based on what they had to prepare on a daily, weekly, monthly, and yearly schedule. This complex rhythm of multitasking required high intelligence and creative finesse.

Every plantation served bread, which is a simple item but easy to ruin. A common recipe for family bread called for the following:

2 quarts of flour.
2 tablespoonfuls of lard or butter.
2 tablespoonfuls of salt.
Enough sponge for a two quart loaf of bread.
Mix with one pint of sweet milk.
Make into rolls and bake with very little fire under the
    oven.[11]

Precise measuring was required for the proper chemical balance of this diet staple. In addition to being accurate in his or her measurements, the cook had to be able to control the temperature of the Dutch oven and the fire. Most recipes also called for "knead[ing] the bread for half an hour without intermission."[12] This labor-intensive food, which was prepared daily, relied on both craft and physical strength.

While the bread was being prepared, the cook would have other short-term items in progress. Fish was consumed on a daily basis and was cooked in multiple ways. The following recipes were Virginia classics:

Fish a la Crème

Boil a firm fish, remove the bones, pick it to pieces. Mix one pint cream or milk with two tablespoonfuls flour, one onion, one-half pound butter (or less), and salt. Set it on the fire and stir until it is as thick as custard. Fill a baking-dish alternately with fish, cracker, and cream. Bake for thirty minutes, use four crackers.[13]

Halibut

Boil one pound halibut, then chop it very fine and add eight eggs well beaten; pepper and salt to taste, then one cup butter. Put it in a stewpan and cook until the eggs are done sufficiently. Serve very hot on toast.[14]

While the halibut recipe was fairly straightforward, the fish a la crème required some skillful techniques. Depending on the type of fish, the bones might be large and easy to pick or small and cumbersome. Picking the bones out of a catfish or a small local shad, perch, or bass would require excellent eyesight and knowledge of the fish's anatomy. Making a custard over the hot fire was another challenging task, since the use of dairy products represented a wild card in hearth cooking. The consistency, temperature, and timing had to be precise; otherwise, the dish would burn, curdle, or fail to set correctly.

In addition to fish, enslaved cooks used oysters in many dishes. Fithian mentioned eating oysters in some fashion almost every day while living at the Carter family plantation. Oysters were readily available in nearby rivers and were caught by both enslaved men and plantation gentry. Similar to enslaved cooks, enslaved fishermen were often sold separately and at higher rates than field laborers.[15] These fishermen would spend their days in Virginia's waterways catching fish and oysters for the main house. Fishermen and cooks worked together to put seafood on the plantation table. Catching seafood could be a challenging task, as was preparing it for guests. Oysters in particular required immediate cooking and intense labor. For example, a basic "Oyster Sauce for Fish" called for the following procedure:

> Scald a pint of oysters, and strain them through a sieve; then wash some more in cold water, and take off their beards; put them in a stew-pan, and pour the liquor over them; then add a large spoonful of anchovy liquor, half a lemon, two blades of mace, and thicken it with butter rolled in flour. Put in half a pound of butter, and boil it till it is melted—take out the mace and lemon, and squeeze the lemon juice into

the sauce; boil it, and stir it all the time, and put it in a boat.[16]

But first the cook had to shuck the oysters (forty to sixty of them to make a pint); this required a hard, sharp tool; a firm and steady hand; and finesse to avoid getting shells in the meat. After forcefully prying open dozens of oysters, the cook then had to sear them over a hot fire, push them through a metal sieve (making a mush), and add items such as floured butter (which, as noted previously, required its own share of labor) and anchovy liquor (another complex recipe). This entire process could take an hour or longer.

Oyster soup was another common meal, consisting of the following ingredients and techniques:

100 oysters.
1 teaspoonful salt.
1 tablespoonful black pepper.
¼ pound butter.
Yolks of three eggs.
1 pint rich milk, perfectly fresh.
3 tablespoonfuls flour.

Separate the oysters from the liquor: put the liquor to boil, when boiled add salt, pepper and butter, then the flour, having previously made it into a batter. Stir all the time. When it comes to a boil add the eggs well beaten, then the milk, and when the mixture reaches a boil, put in the oysters; let them also just boil, and the soup is done. Stir all the time to prevent curdling.[17]

Similar to fish preparation, the cook's attention was constantly focused on the pot of soup. Any slight distraction or mistake would result in a broken soup, a waste of time and ingredients, and an upset mistress.

Another labor-intensive dish, Brunswick stew, was a Virginia staple. Enslaved cooks were familiar with the production and timing of this common dish, which involved a daylong process. Here is one recipe for Brunswick stew:

A shank of beef.
A loaf of bread—square loaf.
1 quart potatoes cooked and mashed.
1 quart cooked butter-beans.
1 quart raw corn.
1½ quart raw tomatoes peeled and chopped.

If served at two o'clock, put on the shank as for soup, at the earliest possible hour; then about twelve o'clock take the shank out of the soup and shred and cut all of the meat as fine as you can. Carefully taking out bone and gristle, and then return it to the soup-pot and add all of the vegetables; the bread and two slices of middling are an improvement to it. Season with salt and pepper to the taste; and when ready to serve, drop into the tureen two or three tablespoonfuls butter.[18]

This classic recipe is a perfect example of how labor was broken down in plantation kitchens. The corn, potatoes, beans, and tomatoes were grown and picked by the field laborers; the meat was slaughtered by the enslaved butcher; and the bread and the stew itself were prepared by the cook. It took an entire labor network to put the dish on the table.

Cooks often had multiple projects running at once and worked from before sunup to well after sundown. A particularly challenging item was sausage. Modern technology (such as the automatic sausage stuffer) has made sausage making somewhat easier, but in early Virginia it was a demanding task. Of the vast number of items made in the kitchen, sausages were by far the most unsanitary. Cooks either acquired pig intestines from the butcher or cut them out of the animal themselves. Then they had to clean the feces out of the entrails by hand, followed by boiling them to get rid of the remainder of the waste. After processing the intestines, the enslaved cooks prepared the minced filling, another labor-intensive assignment that involved hand-chopping the meat and mixing the seasonings. The cooks then stuffed, by hand, the intestines with the meat filling, an exceedingly cumbersome chore.

Cooks were also trained pastry chefs, baking desserts, pies, cakes, and custards for the plantation household. Mistresses kept the alcohol and sugar locked up, but the cooks had partial access to these items. The following recipes are examples of common Virginia desserts:

A Risen Cake

Take three pounds of flour, one and a half of pounded sugar, a teaspoonful of cloves, one of mace, and one of ginger, all finely powdered—pass the whole through a sieve, put to it four spoonsful of good yeast, and twelve eggs—mix it up well, and if not sufficiently soft, add a little milk: make it up at night, and set it to rise—when well risen, knead into it a pound of butter, and two gills of brandy; have ready two pounds of raisins stoned, mix all well together, pour it into a mould of proper size, and bake it in an oven heated as for bread; let it stand till thoroughly done, and do not take it from the mould until quite cold.[19]

A Rich Cake

Take four pounds of Flower [sic][,] 3 pound[s] of Sugar[,] 3 pound[s] of Butter[,] 3 dozen Eggs. Cream your butter then Strain your Eggs to beat, mix it together with the Flower and Sugar. Finely beat nutmegs and the same quantity of mace & a Race of Ginger and near half a pint of Brandy or wine[,] 2 pound and a half of Currants and what quantity of Citron you please, let your oven be hot and bake it near three hours.[20]

Like the previous dishes, these delicacies required timing and attention. But with baking, perfect measurement is essential, as the recipe is like a chemical equation. These recipes unveil the cooks' ability to count and perform educated tasks.

Finally, enslaved cooks were talented wine makers, brewers, and distillers. Many of them brought their knowledge of such arts from West Africa. Their kitchens were full of casks, pot liquors, and brewing beer. Alcohol was a popular beverage, in that it was sterile and healthier than water and provided a pleasant buzz to those who consumed it. The following recipe lays out the technique for making wine:

Be sure to get perfectly ripe fruit for making wine, but do not gather it immediately after rain, as it is watery then and less sweet than usual. Be very careful to stop the wine securely as soon as fermentation ceases, as otherwise it will lose its strength and flavor. Watch carefully to see when fermentation ceases.

The clearest wine is made without straining, by the following process: take a tub or barrel (a flour-barrel for instance), and make a little pen of sticks of wood at the bottom. On top of this pen lay an armful of clean straw. Bore a hole in the side of the tub or barrel as near the bottom as possible, and set it on a stool or box so as to admit of setting a vessel underneath it. After mashing the berries intended for wine, put them on top of the straw, and let the juice drain through it and run through the hole at the side of the tub or barrel into the vessel set beneath to catch it. Be careful to have this vessel large enough to avoid its being overrun. Any open stone vessel not used before for pickle will answer, or a bucket or other wooden vessel may be used. Let the berries remain on the straw and drain from evening till the next morning. Some persons make a slight variation on the process above described by pouring hot water over the berries after putting them on the straw. After the draining is over, an inferior sort of wine may be made by squeezing the berries.

The following process will make wine perfectly clear: to a half-gallon of wine put two wine-glasses of sweet milk, stir it into the wine and pour it all into a transparent half-gallon bottle. Stop it and set it by for twenty-four hours, at the end of which time the wine will be beautifully clear, the sediment settling with the milk at the bottom. Pour off the wine carefully into another bottle, not allowing any of the sediment or milk to get into the fresh bottle. The same directions apply to vinegar.[21]

Prosecco was another common European-inspired beverage that called for similar space and skill. This time-consuming process was essential for the success of plantation balls and dinners, so wine making was a constant activity in the kitchen. Wine was also used as medicine: "Strawberry wine makes a delicious flavoring for syllabub, cake, jelly, etc. And so does gooseberry wine. Dewberries make a prettier and better wine than blackberries, and have all the medicinal virtues of the latter."[22]

Negotiations

Enslaved cooks were at the center of domestic success, and as such, they were able to negotiate some of their labor. Their workload was constant and stressful. At Middleway Plantation in Gloucester County, Virginia, "The servants were never dismissed—their training never ended and they were part of a complex social system."[23] Enslaved cooks found themselves in an exclusive position. Being responsible for producing food made them the most important slaves in the household, which allowed for labor negotiations and individual agency. Cooks and other domestics chose to revolt against expected social behaviors on occasion, which infuriated their mistresses:

> Uncle Bob Iveson was a splendid butler and Mammy's son Daniel Cosby was his assistant and a very young man. I suppose Uncle Bob thought he owned the place because his drunkenness became unbearable. It appears that the butlers were expected to get drunk after the entertainments and this lapse from discipline was overlooked in a measure. When their condition next day was too obvious, the master stormed! But Uncle Bob got drunk at the entertainments and thereby caused mortification. Uncle Bob was demoted to watch over the garden, and Mammy's son Daniel was promoted to pantry.[24]

Uncle Bob clearly acted against the expectations of domestic performance and front-stage behavior. His demotion, a direct result of his dismissal of cultural norms, shows a juncture between community expectation and individual choice. As one author described it, a household's "shared imaginative universe, could shimmer with mutual affection or shatter in mutual antagonism."[25] Mistresses appropriated pride from proper servant etiquette, but this was a two-way exchange. Cooks "owned the kitchen," while mistresses "owned the food" as well as the embarrassment that resulted from poor representations of their protected white cultural world. One can imagine the daily frustrations of enslaved domestics who had to walk that line drawn by white supremacist ideologies and undeniable racial casting. Drinking was an escape, a way to participate in the conspicuous consumption of wealth. Most of all, it was a direct refusal to adhere to the household laws and to resign that self-imposed dignity for a moment and push back against the plantation elite.

In a letter to Rueben Dean, the overseer at Strawberry Hill Plantation, a frustrated Ms. Holladay complained about her domestic help: "Last week little was done, and altho three days the woman was doing nothing, yet yesterday when she could have been milling she was kept to wash in the house, which she might as well of done the days she was idle. If I am to feed, cloth, pay hire for servants, I expect their services."[26] The enslaved woman in question had obviously been hired out from another plantation and had decided she was not going to work. Another example of blatant disregard for their duties is described in this post-emancipation recollection:

Post–Civil War conditions worsened by the hiring of a cook Lishy. She was stupid, roughish, sullen and often neglectful of work that she knew how to do well—but she was never discharged. She had been born and raised in the servants' quarters and when the Negroes drifted away to a near Yankee camp, Lishy was deserted. She was taken into the house and shared the protection afforded my young aunts, remaining on the place. . . . Mistress supervised well sifted flour, and proper proportions of salt and lard. . . . Lishy would sift great mounds of flour; so much for light bread, so much for waffles, so much for biscuit. . . . Remember Lishy you have two quarts of flour. That will make thirty-six good sized biscuit. . . . Grandmother didn't count the biscuit as they come up hot to her pleasant supper table but Lishy thought she did. From my seat behind her at the side table, I could hear her occasional message:—"Tell Lishy her biscuits are getting too small!" . . . Grandmother was safe-guarding Lishy's morals and family interests with a prevision that was second nature. Oh! The elegant thrift of those Southern housewives, more productive of comfort than the most lavish expenditure![27]

Lishy might have been an excellent cook before the war, and her attitude changed afterward; or she might have acted as many enslaved cooks did—taking as much time as they liked. While there was a constant threat of punishment, the mistress was so reliant on the cook that their relationship was controlled in part by the willingness of the enslaved cook to cooperate.

Enslaved cooks often knew more about their jobs than their mistresses did.[28] While the mistress took pride in the food made by the cook, she rarely lingered in the kitchen or visited the smokehouse or outbuildings.[29] She was sometimes subjected to controlling demands from her cook. There are records of cooks telling their mistresses to get out of kitchen, a practice that could occur only in a negotiated relationship.[30]

The only real control the mistress had was her ability to dole out provisions such as sugar, spices, and butter.[31] The smokehouse and dairy were part of the white domestic landscape, and as such, the mistress was in charge of them as well. This contrasts with the management of field laborers, who were controlled by an overseer. Sugar in particular must have demanded extra attention. As we now know, the consumption of sugar has physical and emotional effects, leading to a cycle of craving, desire, and control between the supplier of sugar (mistress) and the producer of sweets (cook).[32] Cooks had the ability to "steal" items, such as raw materials or prepared food, for themselves and their families. The mistresses did not watch their cooks' every movement, so there were frequent opportunities for inconspicuous consumption.

In addition to sneaking food from the white folks' groceries, cooks sometimes turned a blind eye and let bad things happen. On Monday, December 14, 1857, Richard Eppes awoke to find a disturbing scene at his new well: "Much shocked this morning on opening the new well back of the cook's garden to find that some scoundrel had stolen a hog and pitched the entrails and ribs down the well. Could not find who did it."[33] The cook almost certainly would have heard the killing of a hog or the noises associated with a quick butchering, and her silence represented loyalty to the other slaves. This person clearly took the preferred meat and left the intestines and ribs to rot in the well, not bothering to engage in the lengthy process of cleaning the intestines for consumption. The cook, living adjacent to the well, must have turned a blind eye, or perhaps she did it herself.

RESISTANCE

Many enslaved cooks ran away from their plantations. Rachael, who belonged to John Aylett, ran away after three months of cooking for him. He placed a runaway ad in the *Virginia Gazette* reading:

THREE months ago I purchased, from the executors of *Littlebury Hardiman,* a negro woman named RA-CHAEL, formerly Mr. *Hardiman's* cook, since which I have not seen her. I am informed she has a husband at one of Col. *Carter's* quarters on *James* River, through whose benevolence I imagine she is now harboured. Whoever brings her to me, at *Drummond's Neck,* near *Cowels* ferry, shall receive 30s, or 20s if conveyed to *Charles City* prison. I am determined not to dispose of her, and will sue any who entertain her.[34]

Rachael had been sold away from her family and was unable to negotiate her placement, as others were sometimes allowed to do. It is clear by the ad that Mr. Aylett valued her skills and would go to great lengths to recapture her.

In April 1751 a Virginia-born enslaved man named Hercules ran away from his Prince George County plantation. Hercules, a repeat runaway, was known for pretending to be a cook.[35] This notion of posing as a cook speaks to the flexibility granted to some of Virginia's enslaved chefs. Their presence at a market or on a road might be excused, as cooks had more fluid boundaries between their plantations' borders and city centers.

While many enslaved cooks had the power to negotiate their labor, many were abused by their enslavers. Elizabeth Sparks of Mathews, Virginia, remembered her mistress's violence: "She'd give the cook jes' so much meal to make bread fum an' effen she burnt it, she'd be scared to death 'cause they's whup her."[36] Ex-slave Susan Jackson of Fredericksburg recalled the violence on her old plantation, where the perpetrator was the master: "Her ole Marsa, named Allen, treated her jus' like a dog. She was de cook, an' he would beat her if he didn't like what she cooked."[37] Liza Brown recalled that her mother, a plantation cook, had been abused even while pregnant: "When mother was in a pregnant stage, if she happen to burn de bread or biscuits, Missus would order her to the granary, make her take off all her clothes . . . sometimes 'twon' but one piece. After she stripped her stark naked she would beat mother wid a strap."[38] These moments are a stark reminder that no matter how much agency enslaved cooks had, they lived in constant fear of violent abuse.

The skills of enslaved cooks allowed them a certain level of satisfaction, drastically different from other domestics. Their food-centered jobs relied on their senses—smell, taste, sight, touch, and sound—all of which varied from person to person. One person's palate might not be the same as another's, and the ability to not just follow a recipe but actually create food relied on individual tastes and ingenuity. This complex role must have inspired a sense of pride and a level of personal fulfillment. Within the horrors of enslavement, enslaved cooks took ownership of their food and received compliments for their skills. To maintain dignity in an abusive relationship (which slavery was) is to survive. This mixture of pain and joy, work and family, was something enslaved folks held on to and struggled with throughout their lives.[39]

Parenting, Family, and Domestic Relations

Motherhood played out in the kitchen differently than it did in the slave quarters. As noted earlier, enslaved cooks were allowed to share their living space with their partners and their immediate families. Their children either helped them in the kitchen, performing some of the more tedious tasks such as picking stems, shucking corn, and making biscuits, or worked in the main house as servants. This practice of having their children working and living next to them provided a more intimate family setting and carried into the profits of slavery. This is seen in advertisements

for the sale of cooks, along with their children: "SUKEY HAMIL-
TON, cook to the late Govenour, with her youngest daughter, 7
years old."[40] A sale at the Brunswick courthouse included "sundry
NEGROES, among which are two very fine house wenches, and
their children, the wenches can wash and iron, cook.[41] Advertisements in Williamsburg mentioned "a LIKELY young Negro
WENCH, about 25 years of age, she has a child of two months
old, understands cooking, making paste, pickling,"[42] and "a young
cook wench with two children.[43] These ads expose the currency
cooks had and how their children were seen as part of their labor
machine. Because these children helped in the kitchen and contributed to the production of meals, they were valued *with* the
cook. Even when planters sold off their slaves, they often kept
their house servants to preserve domestic stability.

This sort of familial inclusion is also evident in an incident
involving kidnapping. On October 31, 1828, Thomas Spragins received a letter from an angry neighbor, James Wills, accusing him
of breaking into Wills's kitchen and kidnapping the cook Lucy
and her children. He stated, "The peculiarities I need not mention by note."[44] Mr. Wills just wanted his cook and her children
back because, without them, his household was unable to function
as a domestic machine. Why Mr. Spragins kidnapped Lucy and
her children is unknown. Perhaps he was hoping to appropriate
Lucy's skills, or his motive might have been vengeance, and steal-
ing her was the most hurtful thing he could do to his neighbor.
Maybe he was a sexual predator, or perhaps he had a sincere relationship with Lucy.

Descriptions of cooks were provided by travelers such as David Hunter Strother, whose group was passing through Amherst
County. On November 6, 1855, they stopped for a bite to eat,
and Strother's traveling companion Porte Crayon secured them
a meal:

As the roads were heavy, and the chances of finding places of entertainment but few, the driver stopped at an early hour in front of a house of rather unpromising exterior. Porte Crayon, who has a facility of making himself at home everywhere, went to the kitchen with a bunch of squirrels, the spoil of his German rifle. He returned in high spirits. "Girls, we will be well fed here; we are fortunate. I have just seen the cook; not merely a black woman that does the cooking, but one bearing a patent stamped by the broad seal of nature; the type of a class whose skill is not of books or training, but a gift both rich and rare who flourishes her spit as Amphitrite does her trident (or her husband's which is all the same), whose ladle is a royal scepter in her hands, who has grown sleek and fat on the steam of her own genius, whose children have the first dip in all gravies, the exclusive rights to all livers and gizzards, not to mention the breasts of fried chickens—who brazens her mistress, boxes her scallions, and scalds the dogs (I'll warrant there is not a dog on the place with a full suit of hair on him). I was awed to that degree by the severity of her deportment when I presented the squirrels, that my orders dwindled into a humble request, and throwing half a dollar on the table as I retreated I felt my coat-tails to ascertain whether she had not pinned a dishrag to them. In short, she is a perfect she-Czar, and I may never bite another corn-cake if I don't have her portrait tomorrow."[45]

Perhaps this passage is plagued by hyperbole, but it is clear that this particular cook impressed the travelers so much that they documented her both in words and by portrait (see figure 5).

Figure 5. Drawing from *Harper's New Monthly Magazine*, January 1856, 177. (Copy in Special Collections, University of Virginia Library; courtesy of Jerome S. Handler, Virginia Foundation for the Humanities, Slavery Images database)

While many enslaved cooks lived in the kitchen with their biological families, the other enslaved domestic laborers created a family-like community within the plantation home. They worked closely together in the white landscape and developed a sense of camaraderie. Members of this larger catering network, made up of cooks, maids, butlers, and waiters, were known as "the lords of the back-stairs."[46] An early-twentieth-century Virginia memoir revealed the attempt to create actual families among the enslaved: "My grandparents brought wise young heads to the management of their plantation. They wished to encourage intermarriage among their servants, so with that in view for the moral edification of all a premium was offered. Grandfather furnished a cabin for the groom, and grandmother gave a wedding frock and supper to the bride when there was a religious ceremony."[47] This kind of social engineering was intended to create a culture of submissiveness and offered small rewards for couples who felt pressured to marry. At the same time, within every "encouragement," enslaved folks undoubtedly negotiated as much autonomy as they could, considering their situation.

White slaveholding families sometimes had fond feelings for the people they enslaved. They often recalled their enslaved domestic staff with nostalgia: "I can hardly understand myself and it's hard to explain, the great influence of these old family servants. The position was that of old cabinet ministers, only the incoming administration could not get rid of them as they were on the estate for life. Also, they had great weight with all the plantation for the house-servants represented the plantations aristocracy and were revered accordingly."[48] This is the exact tone that solidified the mythical "happy house slave" narrative.

This network of enslaved domestics had their own views on hierarchies and self-pride. The cook, though central to the white family's presentation of itself, did not always receive the same respect from the enslaved community. An elderly Virginia woman recollected this dynamic on her family's plantation: "In every home there were certain dignitaries among the servants, whose authority and personal influence was second only to that of the master and mistress. The mammy was the most important person upstairs, the butler lorded the pantry, the cook queened it in the kitchen and the coachman was law-giver in the stables. Their children swarmed unobtrusively around and were the future lady's maids, seamstresses, pastry cooks, butlers and coachmen. These four dignitaries were part of the administration and jealously guarded their prestige."[49] This dated memory speaks to the cook's "queenly" role, but only in conjunction with the other domestics. The tendency for enslaved folks to appropriate the pride of the plantation was reminiscent of the way the mistress took false credit for the cook's food, thus illustrating the importance of domestic pride and success. In the same memoir, the author described a proud division between the domestics:

> I remember when I was a girl that Daniel Cosby was engaged to preside in the dining room on the occasion of the marriage of one of my aunts. The house was full of guests and Grandfather was famous for his lambs. There were many negro assistants in the kitchen, and when the giving out had to be done, Daniel was consulted as to the proper provision for them. "Don' give 'em none of dat lam' dey won't touch it!" When his own dinner was given out, he said: —"I would like a little lam' please marm, I was raised in the house an' on sheep meat. Dem folks in dat kitchen aint had no raisin' at all and dey don' know nothin'!" There is no scorn in the world equal to the scorn of the house servant for plantation raising.[50]

The use of lamb as a class separator shows the minute social stratifications between the front-stage domestics and those working in the kitchen. We cannot know why the cook and the kitchen laborers would not eat the lamb, but given that they were the ones who prepared it, we might assume that they knew best. Regardless, butlers lived inside the house, which made them feel culturally different from the others, or at least they tried to assert a certain prestige in front of the white folks.

The Kitchen as Crossroads

It is clear that the kitchen was both home and workplace for enslaved cooks. The conditions were complex; though larger than field quarters, the cooks' domain lacked privacy and separation from work. Kitchens were at a crossroads between black and white worlds and performed a unique function on the plantation. The intersecting space of the kitchen was the social center of the plantation community.

Mr. Fithian often mentioned this unique space in his journal. He wrote: "There came about 8 o'clock, a man very drunk, and grew exceedingly noisy and troublesome, and as the evening was cold and stormy Mr. Carter thought it improper to send him away; he was therefore ordered into the kitchen to stay the night."[51] This incident shows the value of the kitchen as a safe harbor for a stranger, yet it also provided security for the Carter family. Leaving the disorderly man in the hands of the cook speaks to the liminal nature of the kitchen quarters. Fithian also recalled that young Harry Carter was continually drawn into the plantation kitchen and played in the other domestic buildings at night: "This evening the Negroes collected themselves into the school room and began to play the fiddle and dance. . . . Harry was among them dancing with his coat off. . . . I dispersed them immediately."[52]

Similarly, in an 1864 letter, Virginia mistress Eleanor Platt wrote, "The children soon ran off to dance in the kitchen as they do every night."[53] This sort of interracial socialization was a constant in the kitchen, especially among the children. Ex-slave Hannah Johnson recalled, "My mother was de cook; her name was Hannah too. Dey was crazy 'bout her. I come up as one of de white chillum—didn' know no difference. We et together at de same table. I slept in de same bed wid de white folks."[54] There was a certain level of fluidity in the interactions between white and black children, and the kitchen acted as a vehicle for these encounters. Sometimes the enslaved children would go into the main house, but usually only if there were a particular reason to do so. Baily Cunningham recalled that "all the work hands ate in the cabins and all the children took their cymblin [squash] soup bowl to the big kitchen and got it full of cabbage soup. Then we were allowed to go [to] the table where the white folks ate and get the crumbs from the table."[55] This sort of psychoemotional action remaps violence onto enslaved children by reinforcing ideas about status, worth, and disrespect of the black body. It is clear that a black child within the white house was cautious and reserved; however, a white child in the kitchen was free of the social constraints of elite culture.

Kitchens were socially active and open spaces. They also served as a formal venue for weddings. The traditional "jumping the broom" ceremony often occurred in the slave quarters, yet the kitchen hosted these occasions as well. On New Year's Eve 1856, Richard Eppes's cooks Emma and Harriet threw a wedding party for John Bird and Patience Anderson in the kitchen. Eppes described the festivities: "The close of the year 1856. Since Christmas we have had nothing to break the monotony of these festival times but a marriage and marriage party between two of the Bermuda negroes John Bird and Patience Anderson married by me in this dining room Sunday December 28th according to the doctrine of the P.E. Church in presence of Mrs. E and Emma, nurse White and the house servants. The party came off the following night Monday in the kitchen given by Harriet and Emma."[56] Two years later, Eppes was involved in another kitchen wedding reception. On Tuesday, December 28, Eppes ordered twenty loaves of bread, $3 worth of cakes, and $3 worth of candy for the slaves. He recorded in his diary: "George our dining room servant was married tonight to a girl belonging to Mrs. Wood by name of Anna. Mrs. Eppes gives them an entertainment in our kitchen."[57] These glimpses into the kitchen's multiple functions illustrate its centrality to both the white and the black communities.

This kind of social interaction can also be seen in the archaeological record. For example, Dixon Plantation in King and Queen County was established sometime in the middle of the eighteenth century by William Dixon and his family. The external kitchen was built in accordance with Virginia's architectural traditions, and it sat adjacent to the house. In 2002 the James River Institute for Archaeology was contracted by the current owner to excavate the remains of the eighteenth-century kitchen, which had burned in the 1760s. After the fire, the occupants had swept the remains into the cellar and the adjacent trash pit. This short-term solution proved to be of long-term value, in that it captured the kitchen in a sort of a time capsule. Rarely are archaeologists able to uncover the entire material world of a past space. The Dixon kitchen is an informative snapshot of mid-eighteenth-century kitchen life and provides a rich archaeological narrative.

By the eighteenth century, the kitchen was the heart of the plantation. The written record documents the importance of the cook's role on the plantation, and the archaeological record supports this and adds textures of daily life that cannot be captured in written documents. The Dixon time capsule tells the story of elite Virginians sharing space with enslaved Afro-Virginians, all within the confines of the kitchen space. Many such kitchens were used for celebrations where the enslaved and white populations mingled. The kitchen as a black landscape within a larger white landscape was a relatively safe social space for the greater plantation community to gather together.

The kitchen was more than just a venue for food production and laundry; this unique space hosted lively receptions, large gatherings, and nightly socials. Games were a significant part of eighteenth-century culture, and the artifacts found at Dixon included an assortment of marbles and unidentified glass objects that were obviously used to play games within the kitchen walls. Frederick Olmsted traveled through Virginia and described White Sulphur Springs as a place that was fully staffed by enslaved blacks and ran dry of beds and food in August. He noted that the whites would go down to the kitchen, where there was banjo playing, and the "darkies in the place stood up and down in the kitchen."[58] These "snapshots" of kitchen life yield a better understanding of these physical spaces as a sort of crossroads for cultural expression and socialization.

Enslaved cooks were not exempt from torture; nor did their high status protect them from mental abuse. They were proud of their food, but they were forced to perform domestic chores that often resulted in physical and emotional trauma. This pride, cycled within performance and pain, was unique to enslaved cooks and resulted in a challenging and stressful existence. The backstage scene was one of uncomfortable working conditions, long hours of labor, and a responsibility that lent itself to negotiation, abuse, and small moments of empowerment.

Three

IN FAME AND FEAR

Exceptional Cooks

Virginia was home to some of the most notorious enslaved cooks in the Atlantic world. Some of them became this nation's first celebrity chefs. Their reputations transcended nation, race, and class, and they were known as the best of the best. Other cooks were well known throughout the colonies and the nation for poisoning their enslavers. Their positions within their owners' households afforded them incredible trust, and they used that trust to terrify and occasionally kill their enslavers. Enslaved cooks in general provided a sense of pride and comfort to white families; the exceptional ones made the news and were central to dinner conversations throughout the South. They represented all that could be, both in fame and in fear.

PRESIDENTIAL CHEFS

George Washington's Mount Vernon was made up of five different farms, all housing their own enslaved communities. The first recorded enslaved cook there was "Old Doll," who came to the estate as part of Martha Washington's dowry. Doll was seventy-eight years old when Martha brought her to Mount Vernon, and her daughter Lucy cooked in the kitchen as well. An enslaved man named Nathan was also listed as a cook; he worked at Mansion House, one of the five farms on the estate. Nathan cooked from at least 1786 to approximately 1795. In addition, Mount Vernon housed a mill and a distillery, where "Old Betty" cooked and taught her son Hanson some very famous recipes:

Hansons [sic] Mode of Making Chicken Broth; the Best in the World

Take a large chicken, kill, scald, pick, clean, & skin it. [P]ut it into a pot with a close cover[.] [P]our in 3 pints of cold water, let it simmer slowly. [I]n half an hour put in a little Thyme. [H]alf an hour after, a tablespoonful of flour & water mixed smooth & stirred in[.] When the bones come thro' the meat, it is done. It must never boil, only simmer very slowly. If a small chicken, 1 quart of water is enough. If you wish it very nourishing—break the bones with a rolling pin before you put it into the pot. Chicken water is the best remedy for Cholera Morbus. [F]irst warm water or weak chamomile tea, then chicken water. So tho't Dr. Jenifer who was celebrated for the cure of that disease.[1]

Hanson's Thin Biscuits

[Take] one quart of flour[,] half a pint of sweet milk[,] one table spoonful of Butter; mix the butter with half the flour, then work in the milk with the flour & butter by degrees, then work in the rest of the flour very well, make the dough stiff. [T]hen roll it hard with the rolling pin 8 or 10 times thin, cut it out with a round tin cutter or tumbler, stick a few holes in each biscuit with a fork, bake in an oven not too hot, slowly; when they break *short*, & you can snap them in half without *bending* they are done.[2]

Hansons [sic] Breakfast Biscuits

Take a quart of dough, add butter the size of a hens [sic] egg, work it up very well so as to mix the butter & dough well, roll it out 3 or 4 times[.] [C]ut it in small pieces, roll them up like an

Egg. [J]ust flatten them a little with the rolling pin, set them by a few minutes to rise, & bake them in a slow oven.[3]

Martha Washington prided herself on her housekeeping skills. She was in charge of hiring the staff, both free and enslaved, who worked for her and her husband. She noted: "There are always two persons . . . in the Kitchen; and servants enough in the house for all needful purposes—These require Instructions in some cases, and looking after in all.—To be trust worthy—careful of what is committed to him—sober and attentive, are essential requisits [*sic*] in any large family, but more so among blacks— many of whom will impose when they can do it."[4] As the nation's first First Lady, her role as mistress was a public one, and one particular enslaved laborer became a fast celebrity.

Chef Hercules

Chef Hercules climbed the ranks to become chef to the first president of the United States. He was born around 1754 and at age sixteen was purchased by George Washington.[5] He remained a house servant for more than a decade before moving into the kitchen. He married a Mount Vernon seamstress named Alice who was owned by Martha Washington and was listed as "lame" in the 1786 inventory. Alice and Hercules had three children: Richmond (born 1776), Evey (born 1784), and Delia (born 1785).[6] Two years after their youngest was born, Alice passed away.[7] In February 1786 Hercules, who was about thirty-two years old at the time, officially became a cook, working alongside another enslaved cook named Nathan.[8] The period between 1787 and 1791 was undoubtedly an anxious one for Hercules. In addition to losing his wife of almost two decades, he was abruptly transferred to the president's house in Philadelphia. He went from being an enslaved cook on a rural Virginia plantation to being the chef of the president of the United States of America in a city known for its vibrant free black community.

Chef Hercules was not the only candidate for head chef. Washington put some thought into deciding who would serve and, in essence, represent him in his new presidential home. He wrote to his secretary Tobias Lear on September 9, 1790:

> In my last I left it with you to decide on the propriety of bringing the Washer women [from New York to Philadelphia]. I do so still. But with respect to Mrs. Lewis [the hired cook] and her daughter, I wish it may not be done, especially as it is in contemplation to transplant Hercules or Nathan from the Kitchen at Mount Vernon to that in Philadelphia; and because the dirty figures of Mrs. Lewis and her daughter will not be a pleasant sight in view (as the Kitchen always will be) of the principal entertaining rooms in our new habitation.[9]

President Washington clearly considered the differences between a hired cook, Mrs. Lewis, and an enslaved one, Chef Hercules. Washerwomen were not as dignified as plantation chefs, and it is clear that Hercules warranted enough respect and trust to trump Mrs. Lewis. It is also obvious that the president of the new nation paid particular attention to appearances. By September 17, 1790, Washington had decided against Mrs. Lewis and her daughter but was still mulling over which of his enslaved cooks to take to Philadelphia: "We have resolved to take one of our Cooks with us—and if upon examining into the matter, it shall be found convenient, I may also take on a boy: at any rate there will be no occasion for Mrs Lewis or her daughter; for a Scullion may always be had in Philadelphia."[10] The boy in question was Hercules's son Richmond, and it can be presumed that the delay was due to Hercules negotiating with Washington to allow Richmond to help in the kitchen. On November 14, 1790, Washington wrote, "If Hercules comes on there will only be wanting one woman in the Kitchen who can be got at any time."[11] Soon after, on November 22, Washington wrote to Lear: "The day is come, and the hour at hand, or very nearly—when our journey will commence for Philadelphia. . . . Austin & Herculas [*sic*] goes on in this days Stage, & will, unquestionably arrive several days before us. Richmond and Christopher embarked yesterday by Water—the former not from his appearance or merits I fear, but because he was the Son of Herculas & his desire to have him as an assistant, comes as a Scullion for the Kitchen."[12] Hercules got his wish: his son Richmond would work in the scullery as Hercules's assistant. Washington's own words reflect his disapproval of Richmond's presence, and he clearly articulates that both merit and looks were essential for those working in the president's home.

In late November 1790 Washington brought Hercules to Philadelphia, where he was enslaved alongside eight others. Earlier, Washington had written to Lear and asked him to order three new hats "with fuller and richer tassels at top than the old ones have."[13] These fancy new hats were for Hercules and for stable hands Giles and Paris, who were regularly on display in the public eye. This exemplifies the importance of "front-stage" slavery, the type that attempted to showcase a civil and dignified form of enslavement. However, the location of this inhumane theater provided a two-way gaze. Virginia's enslaved could be seen by free blacks, northern whites, and Europeans, but they, in turn, were able to witness a kind of freedom unheard of in the Old Dominion.

The presence of Chef Hercules and his fellow bondsmen

stirred things up in Philadelphia. The staff at the president's house was a mixture of wage laborers and slaves who worked alongside each other. Washington hired professional chef John Vicar to cook with Hercules, but Vicar and Washington's relationship did not end well, and the president replaced him with Samuel Fraunces, a well-known New York tavern keeper, in May 1791. Fraunces had been hired sometime between late March and early April to act as steward and work in collaboration with Hercules.[14] By April 17, 1791, Lear noticed that the kitchen was overstaffed and that Fraunces's position might be unnecessary. Lear wrote to Washington, "Was it not for the aid which is expected from Fraunces in the Cookery, I should rather have objected to his coming than otherwise."[15] He went on to say that Mrs. Washington was directing him on the business of housekeeping and that if the present cook (Vicar) quit, Hercules would do. Finally, Lear mentioned that Hercules's son Richmond would be returning to Mount Vernon at the first opportunity and that Hercules supported this change.[16] The president's kitchen was quite the scene, and it seemed that Hercules—the only enslaved laborer in the kitchen—was on the verge of climbing the ranks.

By May 1791, both Vicar and Richmond were gone, leaving Hercules as the head cook under Fraunces's direction. But something important was happening behind the scenes. One week after Lear advised Washington about the new arrangements, attorney general Edmund Randolph formally warned the president (through Lear) that his enslaved laborers would become free if they stayed in Philadelphia. In 1780 the Pennsylvania legislature had passed an Act for the Gradual Abolition of Slavery that allowed any enslaved person to be automatically manumitted after six consecutive months of residence in the state.[17] This undoubtedly caused much angst in the president's house. As early as April 12, 1791, Washington was trying to resolve this situation and proposed a covert scheme that benefited only himself and his family. He wrote to Lear, "If upon taking good advise [*sic*] it is found expedient to send them [enslaved laborers] back to Virginia, I wish to have it accomplished under pretext that may deceive both them and the Public, and none I think would so effectually do this, as Mrs. Washington coming to Virginia next month."[18] Washington was clearly willing to deceive both the public and his enslaved servants as to the reason for their return to his Virginia plantation.

Washington executed his plan accordingly and sent his enslaved staff back to Virginia to avoid losing them to freedom. There was an exception, however: Hercules and another enslaved man, Austin, would return to Philadelphia after the staged visit home. Lear aided Washington in this deception: "I shall propose to Hercules, as he will be wanted at home in June when you return there, to take an early opportunity of going thither, as his services here can now be very well dispenced [*sic*] with, and by being at home before your arrival he will have it in his power to see his friends—make every necessary preparation in his Kitchen & as he must return when you do to this place."[19]

Since Washington was traveling at the time, there was no need for a full kitchen staff at the president's house in Philadelphia. Specifically, Hercules's skills would not be required until the president's planned return. There was also an ulterior motive for the move back to Virginia: to test the loyalty of Washington's slaves. Lear observed, "If Hercules should decline the offer which will be made him of going home, it will be a pretty strong proof of his intention to take the advantage of the law at the expiration of six months."[20] One of Washington's critical expectations of a cook was honesty, and Lear specifically mentioned these requirements: "The qualifications necessary, besides skill in the business, are honesty, sobriety, and good dispositions."[21] Presumably, Hercules had all three qualities, as he had been chosen to serve the president in Philadelphia. This loyalty test was more than an assessment of flight risk; it was a measure of the overall integrity of the president's trusted cook. Hercules agreed to return to Mount Vernon, initially without question.

Within a month after learning of his upcoming temporary transfer, Hercules caught wind of Washington's real agenda. Lear informed the president of this complicated situation:

> In my letter of the 22d of [M]ay I mentioned that Hercules was to go on to Mount Vernon a few days after that. When he was about to go, somebody, I presume, insinuated to him that the motive for sending him home so long before you was expected there, was to prevent his taking advantage of a six month's residence in this place. When he was possessed of this idea he appeared to be extremely unhappy—and altho' he made not the least objection to going; yet, he said he was mortified to the last degree to think that a suspicion could be entertained of his fidelity or attachment to you. [A]nd so much did the poor fellow's feelings appear to be touched that it left no doubt of his sincerity—and to shew [sic] him that there were no apprehensions of that kind entertained of him, Mrs Washington told him he should not go at that time; but might remain 'till the expiration of six months and then go home—to prepare for your arriv[a]l there. He has accordingly continued here 'till this time, and tomorrow takes his departure for Virginia.[22]

Hercules, who had been so close to freedom, left Philadelphia via stagecoach on June 3, 1791, and returned to the plantation where he had been enslaved since the age of sixteen.

Meanwhile, the president's house was still in professional

turmoil. Fraunces took charge of the kitchen that had previously been run by Vicar. Lear clearly had some big personalities on his hands, and he wrote an animated missive to Washington describing Fraunces's ego:

> Fraunces arrived here on Wednesday, and after signing his Articles of Agreement—going over the things in the house & signing an inventory thereof, entered upon the duties of his station. I think I have made the agreement as full, explicit & binding as any thing of the kind can be. In the Articles prohibiting the use of wine at his table—and obliging him to be particular in the discharge of his duty in the Kitchen & to perform the Cooking with Hercules—I have been peculiarly pointed. He readily assented to them all (except that respecting Hercules, upon which he made the following observation—"I must first learn Hercules' abilities & readiness to do things, which if good, (*as good as Mrs. Read's*) will enable me to do the Cooking without any other *professional* assistance in the Kitchen; but this experiment cannot be made until the return of the President when there may be occasion for him to exert his talents"—)—and made the strongest professions of attachment to the family, & his full determination to conduct in such a manner as to leave no room for impeachment either on the score of extravagance or integrity. All these things I hope he will perform.[23]

This passage highlights the intersection of race, class, and pure culinary ego. Fraunces demanded the opportunity to test Hercules's abilities before agreeing to the terms of his employment. He mentioned Mrs. Read, who in other accounts was cited for her mediocrity, high financial cost, and lack of integrity above anything else. Fraunces's mixed racial heritage, free status, high class, and ego undoubtedly added more complexity to that Philadelphia kitchen.

Hercules returned to the kitchen in Philadelphia after a brief visit home. Account books show that he and Austin, Washington's footman and waiter, were friends and took to the town when they had the time. Hercules spent six years living and laboring in Philadelphia and became well known in the city.

George Washington Parke Custis (Washington's stepgrandson whom he and Martha adopted) recalled Hercules's charm and flamboyance in a detailed and telling passage worthy of repetition here:

> The chief cook would have been termed in modern parlance, a celebrated *artiste*. He was named Hercules, and familiarly termed Uncle Harkless. Trained in the mysteries of his part from early youth, and in the balmy days of Virginia, when her thousand chimneys smoked to indicate the generous hospitality that reigned throughout the whole length and breadth of her wide domain, Uncle Harkless was, at the period of the first presidency, as highly accomplished a proficient in the culinary art as could be found in the United States. He was a dark-brown man, little, if any, above the usual size, yet possessed of such great muscular power as to entitle him to be compared with his namesake of fabulous history.
>
> The chief cook gloried in the cleanliness and nicety of his kitchen. Under his iron discipline, woe to his underlings if speck or spot could be discovered on the

tables or dressers, or if the utensils did not shine like polished silver with the luckless wights who had offended in these particulars there was no arrest of punishment, for judgment and execution went hand in hand. . . .

The steward, and indeed the whole household, treated the chief cook with much respect, as well for his valuable services as for his general good character and pleasing manners.

It was while preparing the Thursday or Congress dinner that Uncle Harkless shone in all his splendor. During his labors upon this banquet he required some half-dozen aprons, and napkins out of number. It was surprising the order and discipline that was observed in so bustling a scene. His underlings flew in all directions to execute his orders, while he, the great master-spirit, seemed to possess the power of ubiquity, and to be everywhere at the same moment.

When the steward [Fraunces] in snow-white apron, silk shorts and stockings, and hair in full powder, placed the first dish on the table, the clock being on the stroke of four, "the labors of Hercules" ceased. . . .

While the masters of the republic were engaged in discussing the savory viands of the Congress dinner, the chief cook retired to make his toilet for an evening promenade. His perquisites from the slops of the kitchen were from one to two hundred dollars a year. Though homely in person, he lavished the most of these large avails on dress. In making his toilet his linen was of unexceptional whiteness and quality, then black silk shorts, ditto waistcoat, ditto stockings, shoes

highly polished, with large buckles covering a considerable part of the foot, blue cloth coat with velvet collar
and bright metal buttons, a long watch-chain dangling
from his fob, a cocked hat, and gold-headed cane com-
pleted the grand costume of the celebrated dandy (for
there were dandies in those days) of the presidents
kitchen. . . .

Thus arrayed, the chief cook invariably passed out at
the front door, the porter making a low bow, which was
promptly returned. Joining his brother-loungers of the
pave, he proceeded up Market street, attracting considerable attention, that the street being, in the old times, the
resort where fashionables "did most congregate." Many
were not a little surprised on beholding so extraordinary
a personage, while others who knew him would make a
formal and respectful bow, that they might receive in return a salute of one of the most polished gentlemen and
the veriest dandy of nearly sixty years ago.[24]

As Custis's passage illustrates, Hercules used his skills to negotiate a lifestyle not available to him at Mount Vernon. As the president's cook living in a northern city, he had the ability to roam
free in high style and interact with the public; he earned such
respect that other servants bowed at his presence. It is possible
that this lifestyle made Washington's political shenanigans tolerable for the time being. But Hercules was also subversive, and the
more connections he made in Philadelphia, the easier his eventual
escape would be.

This manipulation was the ultimate "puttin' on the massa"—
a phrase used by enslaved African Americans to describe the
trickster tactics they employed to resist enslavement. Field hands
acted dumb, secretly broke tools, and faked illnesses to avoid la-

bor. Punishment was always a threat, but enslaved folks were resilient and employed various forms of resistance in order to survive. Enslaved domestics were no different, but their tactics rested on front-stage desires, the white gaze, and the performance of class. Hercules epitomized this type of resistance; he was respected and even became famous within both the enslaved and the free communities. His position allowed him to meet world leaders, abolitionists, and countless free blacks. His skills were revered throughout the Atlantic world, and he undoubtedly had clandestine offers of paid employment and ultimate freedom.

Chef Hercules remained in Philadelphia until at least 1795, when his name appeared in the account books as needing pills. He would have been about forty-one years old and might have been experiencing some serious health issues. By November 1796, records show that Hercules was back at Mount Vernon and working in the garden shoveling manure—a far cry from his highly dignified position in Philadelphia. It is unclear why Hercules returned to Mount Vernon a year or so before Washington's term ended. Perhaps his health was an issue and he wanted to be near his children. Richmond had been getting into mischief during this period, and Washington had written to his farm manager about him: "I hope Richmond was made an example of, for the Robbery he committed on Wilkes Saddle bags[.] I wish he may not have been put upon it by his father [Hercules] (although I never had any suspicion of the honesty of the latter) for the purpose perhaps of a journey together. This will make a watch, without its being suspected by, or intimated to them, necessary; nor w[oul]d I have these suspicions communicated to any other lest it should produce more harm than good."[25] Hercules had always looked out for his son, and perhaps he felt the need to return and mentor him and his other children, after being gone for several years.

A few months later, on February 22, 1797 (George Washington's birthday), Hercules finally escaped to freedom.[26] Washington traditionally gave his enslaved domestic laborers gifts on his birthday, so the timing of Hercules's escape was fitting. He had spent years cultivating connections and developing a highly respectable reputation. He had played along with Washington's devious skirting of the manumission law in Pennsylvania only to eventually run off into the night and take his freedom, bidding a triumphant good-bye to his enslaver.

This particular loss deeply upset Washington, but it was celebrated by those Hercules left behind. Washington attempted to locate Hercules by all possible means, offering a reward for his return. After almost a year of investigation, Washington was notified by Frederick Kitt: "Since your departure [from Philadelphia] I have been making distant enquiries about Herculas [*sic*] but did not till about four weeks ago hear anything of him and that was only that [he] was in town[;] neither do I yet know where he is, and that will be very difficult to find out in the secret manner necessary to be observed on the occasion. I shall however use the utmost exertions in my power, and hereafter inform you of my success."[27]

Hercules returned to Philadelphia, where he undoubtedly planned to live. All those trips between Philadelphia and Mount Vernon, devised to keep him in bondage, had inadvertently introduced Hercules to a network of sympathetic and capable allies who aided his eventual escape. Hercules surely knew the routes, the people, and the politics of navigating between the two cities. His escape was brilliant and, ironically, facilitated by Washington's refusal to set him free.

There are no records indicating that Hercules remained in Philadelphia for the rest of his life; in fact, there are clues that he may have left the country. There is a portrait at the Museo Thyssen-Bornemisza in Madrid, Spain, that is labeled "Portrait of the sup-

Figure 6. Portrait of George Washington's cook (circa late 1700s). Oil on canvas, presumably by Gilbert Stuart, Museo Thyssen-Bornemisza, Madrid, Spain.

posed cook of George Washington," presumably painted by Gilbert Stuart (see figure 6). The details of this painting are under scrutiny, and it may have been created anywhere from 1773 to the early 1800s. In any case, it is probable that Hercules returned to Philadelphia and, through his vast connections, was eventually employed by a European abolitionist and lived the remainder of his life as a free man in a free country.

Back at Mount Vernon, where Washington returned after his second term, they were in dire need of a cook. Specifically, he wanted Hercules and was unwilling to buy another enslaved cook to take that role.[28] By 1801, Martha Washington had hired a paid white cook, and the family finally gave up the search for Hercules.[29] Hercules's children remained enslaved even after Washington's death; they were dower slaves who belonged to Martha and were therefore ineligible for willed manumission. Hercules's son Richmond and his daughters Delia and Evey were sent to labor on Washington's River Farm. After Martha's death in 1802, many of the Mount Vernon slaves, including Delia and Evey, were sold to Lawrence Lewis of Woodlawn Plantation.[30] Richmond was sold to Eliza Parke Custis Law.[31] But years before their departure, in April 1797, Frenchman Louis-Philippe had visited Mount Vernon and learned of the Hercules situation: "The general's [Washington's] cook ran away, being now in Philadelphia, and left a little daughter of six at Mount Vernon. Beaudoin ventured that the little girl must be deeply upset that she would never see her father again; she answered, *'Oh! sir, I am very glad, because he is free now.'*"[32]

Chef James Hemings

James Hemings was owned by Thomas Jefferson, and his story is both triumphant and tragic. He is without question the most well-known enslaved cook in America, and scholars have dedicated significant efforts to studying his life.[33] While no one knows what happened to Hercules after his escape, Hemings's ultimate fate was revealed in a letter from William Evans to Jefferson: "[I] am so sorry to inform you that the report respecting James Hemings having committed an act of Suicide is true, I have made every enquiery at the time his melancholy circumstance took place, the result of which was, that he had been delirious for some days previous to having commited the act, and it is as the General opinion that drinking too freely was the cause."[34]

Chef Hemings's story is often celebrated in the shadows of Jefferson worship, but his tale of misfortune is rarely examined. The triumph and tragedy of Hemings's life speak to the complex nature of enslaved domestics who lived and worked at the crossroads of freedom. Many enslaved cooks had reputations for being drunks, and this was undoubtedly due to both their easy access to liquor and the social stresses of being slaves yet having constant contact with the free world.

While Monticello might have been the epitome of the planter class, many other well-to-do Virginians invested in their cooks as well. Chefs were appraised at significantly higher rates than other domestic laborers. For instance, William Marshall of Fredericksburg described his chef as "an excellent cook about 35 years of age, and inferior to none."[35]

As one of the chefs at Monticello, Hemings was under the direction of a male planter rather than a white housewife, and he quickly rose to celebrity status. He was not the only enslaved cook at Monticello, but his path to fame set him apart from the others. He worked alongside another enslaved cook named Ursula Granger and was followed in that role by his brother Peter, Edith Fossett, and a woman named Fanny. These cooks created the sophisticated meals that Jefferson demanded and were unmatched in skill and execution. Ursula's son Isaac Jefferson recalled that his mother made $7 a month as Jefferson's cook. She was also a wet nurse and nanny to the Jefferson children.[36] She represented the more common type of enslaved cook, whose position was fluid enough to include general domestic duties.

In contrast, James Hemings's skills as a chef brought him

great fame and respect. Born in 1767, Hemings grew up as an en-slaved domestic on the plantation of John Wayles in Charles City County. He and many of his family members became Jefferson's property when they were willed to him after Wayles's death, and Hemings moved to Monticello in 1774. He was sent to Paris in 1784, where Jefferson wanted him to learn French cooking tech-niques. Formal French training, though presumably highly de-sired by planters, was risky. The freedom gained by traveling to France presented the opportunity for escape, but this potential risk did not outweigh Jefferson's desire for a French-trained chef. Hemings immediately picked up the French language and was soon speaking it better than Jefferson. He was thrown into some of the most popular kitchens in Paris and benefited from the men-torship of Adrien Petit, Jefferson's maître d'hôtel.[37]

While residing at the Hotel de Langeac, Hemings trained under world-renowned chefs. He undoubtedly experienced a sense of freedom in a land where slavery had been abolished. Hemings then followed Jefferson back to the States and labored in Philadel-phia. It is unknown whether Hemings and Hercules were friends, but they certainly crossed paths or at least knew of each other's fame. In 1793, after almost a decade of cooking French food for Jefferson and his guests, Hemings negotiated an emancipation contract, with one stipulation being that he train his brother Pe-ter to cook in the same style. James returned to Monticello, and within two years he had fulfilled his contract.

By 1796, Hemings was a free man. Like Hercules, he was drawn to Philadelphia, which was a familiar place where he had made some professional connections during his tenure in the city. He is rumored to have traveled to Europe and had plans to go back to Spain—another eerie parallel with the presumed path of Hercules. But Hemings had a hard time finding paid work, even in Philadelphia. Race trumped class, and as a free black man, he was locked out of the jobs he was qualified for. Like Hercules, he returned to Virginia in shame. Unable to gain employment, he returned to Monticello to be near his family members who remained in bondage and to work, as a paid man, for his former master. After enjoying conditional freedom, high status, and international fame, this must have caused him incredible angst. Hemings's plan to work as a free man failed, however. Like many enslaved cooks, he was an alcoholic, and in October 1801 Hemings drank himself to death while residing in Baltimore.

James's protégé and younger brother Peter Hemings cooked for the Monticello table for years after taking over as head chef. Though his culinary skills did not equal those of his brother, Peter became well known for his brewing. He remained at Monticello while two other enslaved cooks, Edith Fossett and a woman known only as Fanny, accompanied Jefferson to Washington as his presidential chefs. Edith worked for Jefferson for almost fifty years and was reportedly his favorite cook. She was trained in formal French-style cooking and was sent to Washington, DC, to work under Jefferson's head chef, Honore Julien. The White House hosted three dinners a week, all of which required the utmost sophistication and execution. Meanwhile, Edith's husband Joseph Fossett and their children remained at Monticello, which made the young cook anxious and eager to return home. In 1806 Joseph ran away from Monticello to visit Edith in Washington, and Jefferson had him jailed and returned as soon as he was caught. The material benefits of cooking for the president were heavily outweighed by the harshness of human bondage. Edith and Fanny returned to Monticello with Jefferson in 1809 and took over Peter's role as the plantation cooks. The Fossett family was sold during the infamous July 4, 1827, auction of Jefferson's slaves. Edith and her two youngest children were bought by Jessee Scott, a free black in Charlottesville. Joseph was freed that same day but had no means to purchase his family.[38]

Fanny, who worked with Edith in the White House kitchen, was also formally trained in Washington. She was a teenager during her tenure at the White House and was married to a man named Davy. Their relationship was continually jeopardized by Jefferson's overseer Nathaniel Bacon, who threatened to sell them away from each other. Fanny was another victim of the 1827 auction and was separated from her family and friends.

Presidential chefs, though gifted in terms of popularity, were vulnerable as well. Whether dealing with the psychological stress of existing in such a complicated social space or the fear of abuse or sale, they achieved incredible status within the bonds of enslavement yet remained bound to the kitchen and the demands of their enslavers.

Notorious Poisoners

While Hercules and Hemings were gaining fame, other enslaved cooks were inciting fear among the southern white elite, as tales of poisoning spread though their circles. West African healers were commonly used by both blacks and whites in colonial and antebellum Virginia. Enslaved cooks were often given the task of mixing certain medicines, such as tonics, that were used by white families. The difference between medicine and poison is dosage, and as a result, many cooks and healers found themselves "poisoning" folks both intentionally and unintentionally. By 1748, Virginia had passed a law stating, "if any negroe, or other slave, shall prepare, exhibit, or administer any medicine whatsoever, he, or she so offending, shall be adjudged guilty of felony, and suffer death without benefit of clergy."[39] There were exceptions to this rule, as many Virginia families relied on and trusted their healers and cooks to administer such medicines. One might assume that poisoning was more commonly done by women; however, between 1705 and 1865, only 15 percent of these enslaved convicts (18 of 118) were women. Ten of them likely acted alone, while eight had male accomplices.[40]

In addition to making medicines, cooks were responsible for making salves, ointments, remedies, and other household products such as ammonias and dyes.[41] Salve was made by taking "mutton suet[,] turpentine, barren soil, melobonet, parsley, elder bark, Night Shade, and bees wax and adding a little honey and brown sugar to it over a slow fire." Similarly, "mouth water" was made by "tak[ing] Pine Buds, Spanish Oak bark, Alder bark, Persimmon bark, and Sage, boil it in a Bell Metal in weak vinegar, after it boils well take out the ingredients and add Allum Salt Petre and Honey [and] simmer it over a slow fire until its a Syrup." Ointments were made with "lavender[,] Sassafras Bark[,] Chamomile Feather[,] free Mullen Buds & Sage, a pound of Lard to a half pint of Brandy[.] Simmer it over a slow fire, when the strength is sufficient pour off the Herbs, ring them dry[.] [T]his ointment will keep a year or two—get the ingredients in August."[42]

Because they practiced the art of medicinal creation, enslaved cooks had knowledge of and access to poisons such as deadly nightshade and belladonna.[43] Their position of trust as the feeders and nourishers of the plantation household made for a very tangled power relationship. It is also essential to note that the majority of enslaved Afro-Virginians were Igbo who had brought their knowledge of both poisoning and foodways with them from Africa.[44] Igbo were well known for their understanding of herbs and poisons, as well as their familiarity with supernatural powers. Historian Douglas B. Chambers argues that "the use of poison especially evokes a different matrix of meaning rooted in African conceptions of efficacy."[45]

The first record of an enslaved person being convicted of poisoning refers to a woman named Eve. On August 19, 1745, Eve successfully poisoned her enslaver, Peter Montague of Orange County, by polluting his milk. She pleaded not guilty but was convicted by the court and sentenced to be "drawn upon a hurdle to the place of execution, and be there burnt."[46] This form of public execution was reserved for the most unacceptable acts in an attempt to deter similar crimes.

Between 1740 and 1785, poisoning was second only to theft as the most tried crime in Virginia.[47] Between 1706 and 1785, thirty-five of the eighty-five slaves convicted of murder used poison to kill their victims. The first convicted poisoner to be executed was Cuffy Coleman of Caroline County, who was hanged in 1750; followed by Hampton Payne of Bedford County in 1756; Peter Wiley of Caroline County in 1762; Peter Phillips of Caroline County in 1763; Taffy Ware and Dick Harrison of Goochland in 1765; four unnamed slaves in 1767 in Alexandria; and Hudson and Randolph of Prince Edward County in 1770.

The first female slave hanged for poisoning was Judith Harrison, who went to the gallows on June 16, 1772. Cesar Carrington of Cumberland was hanged on January 21, 1773, followed by Dollan Reynolds on February 4, 1786, in Lunenburg, and Randolph on July 21, 1788. In Nottoway County on New Year's Day 1790, two enslaved men, Isaac Thornton and Mark Bolling, were hanged for poisoning. Three years later, a man named Harry Key was hanged on January 11, 1793, in Henrico County, followed by Mingo Corbin of Middlesex on May 30, 1794, and Joe Crenshaw of Lunenburg on August 1, 1795. Allen and Reuben Mason were hanged on January 30, 1795, in Sussex. On July 20, 1798, a man named Ralph Strother was executed in Frederick. Four years later, Punch Wade was hanged on February 26, 1802, in Prince

Edward County; a few days later, on March 2, Bob Steinbridge was hanged in Lunenburg. The following year a man and a woman, Chastity and George Lawson of Virginia Beach, were executed together on January 28, 1803. The third female hanged for poisoning was Fanny Goode from Charlotte County, who died on February 28, 1806. Billy Atkinson was hanged in Nottoway County on May 29, 1807, and ten years later Daniel Bransford of Cumberland County was hanged on January 31, 1817. Delp Mitchell of Louisa was hanged on July 26, 1818, and another couple, Renah and Fanny Dawson of Prince Edward, were hanged together on January 5, 1832.

Two more enslaved women—Eliza Griffin and Roberta Ezell, who worked together in Brunswick—were convicted and hanged on January 12, 1849. Richard Nichols was hanged on April 9, 1859, in Henry, followed a month later by Dow and Harry Nichols, who were hanged on May 17. In 1860 three enslaved men—Colin Johns and Dick and John Spencer from Lunenburg—were convicted of poisoning and hanged on November 9. These three men were the last slaves found guilty of poisoning in the state of Virginia. Post-emancipation records show a striking absence of poisoning convictions, suggesting that the crime was associated with resistance to enslavement.[48]

By the mid-nineteenth century, white enslavers in Virginia were living in a culture of fear. The institution of slavery was being challenged, fueled by repeated uprisings throughout the Atlantic world. Many enslaved African Americans risked punishment to resist their condition, and poisoning was a well-known tactic used by enslaved domestics to kill or harm their enslavers. This often led to criminal charges, as it did in the 1834 Essex County case against four slaves—Shadrach Wilkins, Warner, Tabby, and Mary—who were charged with the attempted murder of Dr. Augustus Roy and his wife Lucy. One of the key witnesses was an enslaved woman named Harriet, who resided in the kitchen. She testified that the defendant Warner had come into the kitchen after supper to ask for a vial and had remarked that "once he was done with it, it would never be fit for anything again."[49]

Just that morning, Warner had attempted to escape, but he had been caught and returned to the plantation. Later, Warner stood on the steps leading to the kitchen loft, asked Harriet what kind of "root" was in the vial, and stated his intent to use it to "fix them," referring to the doctor and his wife. Warner and Tabby, who cooked for the white family, spoke freely in front of Harriet, discussing the type of root and how long it would take to steep. Tabby and Warner considered putting the root in rice, but then Tabby suggested milk, which was easily accessible and a sure way to kill the couple. Tabby then recommended that Warner take some of the root and place it at the Roys' door, which, according to their beliefs, would prevent the master and mistress from using their limbs to hurt them. Tabby was undoubtedly a root worker, and as a cook, she held great power in both the enslaved community and the white family.[50]

Warner and Tabby soon realized that Harriet might divulge their plot, so they threatened to kill her too, if she did. They hoped to have their enslavers, along with the overseer Mr. Newbill, "dead by Monday morning" and buried in the Richmond graveyard. Harriet nevertheless told her master, at which point the kitchen was searched and the vial of root powder, along with papers containing powdered cobalt, hemlock, and hug root, was found, proving an intent to kill the Roys. During the trial, Warner explained that he planned to murder the couple and the overseer because they had whipped him, which he believed warranted murder.[51] The defendants were found guilty and sentenced to be hanged in a public square; however, the governor issued a reprieve and ordered them banished from the country. They were subsequently sold to John McMurry and John B. Williamson, who agreed to take them out of the country, and Dr. Roy received $1,050 in compensation for the sale.[52] At the height of the domestic slave trade, this was the most beneficial option for slaveholders, as it yielded a profit. But it begs the question as to the role of the African Colonization Society and the complicated moral dilemmas that plagued Virginia's elite.

In September 1834 the Pope family of Southampton County petitioned for their slave Charlotte to be sold off the plantation and sent out of the county. They stated that Charlotte "hath become ungovernable and dangerous to the family, threatening to destroy them by poison or otherwise."[53] Such fear was intense during this period, as Nat Turner had led his rebellion just three years earlier. This particular threat, coupled with the trusting yet hinged relationships between cooks and their mistresses, undoubtedly resulted in a unique power dynamic.

Phillip Fithian recorded in his diary the details of an attempted murder on a nearby plantation: "Ben retuned about seven from Westmorland court house—he informed us that Mr. Sorrels Negroes had their trial there today, concurring their accusation of entering their masters house in the night and with an intention to murder him. It was proved (so far as negro evidence will go) that the brother of this Sorrels early last spring bribed some negroes to poison his brother and when that diabolical attempt could not succeed he has since tried to persuade them to murder him!"[54]

Similarly, in April 1849 an enslaved man named Billy was charged with poisoning his owner, Thomas Wilcox, at North Bend Plantation in Charles City County. Ten years later, another house servant was charged with poisoning Wilcox's son.[55]

Poisoning was perceived as such a threat that an 1853 medical conference in Richmond, Virginia, dedicated significant attention to the topic. A highlight of the discussion was a case in

Hanover in which enslaved folks had put arsenic in the ice cream of the Shelton family.[56]

The idea of poisoning went hand in hand with food production, as enslaved cooks had access to their potential victims' food. Although relatively rare, this was one of the many modes of resistance practiced by enslaved folks, and one wonders why more cooks didn't try to poison their masters. Clearly, they had access to poison and to food, and they had the trust of their enslavers—the ideal situation for murder. Perhaps their roles as cooks provided them with enough collateral power to negotiate their living conditions and treatment. The mistress's reputation was largely based on the cook's labor, and this twisted relationship involved a certain level of negotiation and covert power struggles. In one way or another, enslaved cooks were notorious throughout Virginia. Presidential chefs popularized French food, uplifted the presidential table, and experienced enslavement in a distinct manner. A number of plantation cooks poisoned their enslavers. These exceptional cooks represented two extremes along a spectrum of possibilities that tempted many enslaved folks to act on their desires—either to find dignity in slavery or to kill their abusers.

Four

IN DINING

Black Food on White Plates

On November 26, 1827, Virginia housewife Mary Randolph wrote to her sister describing the recent accomplishments of her mother's household: "Mother had a banquet and everything went off to perfection . . . I am very anxious for mother to give a ball, which she has promised me to do as soon as the servants and Mrs. Randolph, who is quite sick, recover. She has promised to invite 250 people."[1] Mary was delighted by the success of her mother's event and was eager to put on an even more elaborate and grandiose one. This sort of entertaining was typical in eighteenth- and nineteenth-century plantation culture, as the physical isolation of the planters' homes created a social network of at-home mistresses who planned some of Virginia's most famous parties. These occasions revolved around the production, presentation, and consumption of meals, and the mistress took pride in her self-proclaimed central role. By the mid-eighteenth century, Virginia hospitality was a well-known regional and cultural standard. "Virginia . . . has always been famed for the style of her living . . . she became noted among the colonies for the princely hospitality of her people and for the beauty and richness of their living."[2]

Behind every meal and in the shadow of every mistress was an enslaved cook who was responsible for creating these lavish dinners. These cooks existed within a complex social space created by racialized and gendered ideologies and fueled by the mistress's domestic needs. This environment, similar to a stage, relied on props and actors, on the performance of domestic rituals, and on stringent social class mores. The relationship was built on status roles, negotiation, and the constant threat of violence. The front-stage behavior was that seen by the guests, and it depended on the mistress's performance as "hostess supreme." The back-stage behavior was what happened before the guests arrived, behind the kitchen door and often between mistress and cook. This chapter considers the front stage, filled with abundant gourmet food, ball gowns, liquor, and music, and it examines the cook's role in plantation social culture.

Entertainment was entangled with a paternalistic society and a system of chattel slavery. This created a particular kind of labor structure in which both the mistresses and the enslaved cooks held unique positions in the plantation household. Elite white women functioned within the patriarchy, but they carved out a gendered space in their highly organized and segmented households. Within this space they had the power to control enslaved domestics, on whom they relied for their social elevation.

Elite white Virginians excelled at the social arts and created a cult of plantation hospitality during the eighteenth century. Between 1740 and 1765, Virginia experienced a fluorescence of luxury; material richness was demonstrated by an abundance of silks, linens, jewels, and metals.[3] Most significantly, there was a transformation in the foodways, dining culture, and social expectations of the elite. Dining and dining rooms became a mode of and space for conspicuous consumption. Food became cuisine, and the sophistication of edible fare was central to the perception of wealth. This generation brought a distinction to their dining rooms that broke from the habits of their frugal forefathers.[4] A typical supper consisted of eight or ten large dishes, a course of pastries, and a final course of nuts, fruit, and preserves.[5]

The construction and separation of private and public spaces within plantation homes reflected eighteenth-century ideas about multiple publics and gendered spaces.[6] The creation of gendered publics in mansion construction acted as both mirrors and metaphors for colonial society.[7] Elite Virginians desired gentility and attempted to perform with refinement at every occasion.[8] "Ornate rooms signaled wealth and taste, and therefore social superiority, as the wealthy invested their objects and their homes with meanings, expressed through an encoded polite behavior, which, it has been argued, sharpened class distinctions."[9] Many Virginians "counted chairs" to gauge the wealth of a planter and his family. The more chairs a home had, the more people it could entertain, placing it high on the social ladder.[10]

The idea of public space was seen in many aspects of planter society. The plantation home acted as a controlled public space, in contrast to a tavern or coffeehouse, where anyone might be present. In rural Virginia, plantations were the epicenter of socialization, as they were isolated and located miles from urban life. Some scholars have argued that women lost some of their control over the home and were moved to the periphery of the house's functional purpose.[11] As described in chapter 1, the compartmentalization of rooms led to a separation of gendered spaces. However, upon a closer examination of the function of food as a social measure, it can be argued that the roles of the mistress and the cook lay at the heart of social success, thus putting women much closer to the center of plantation management. When women left their homes under the care of their husbands, they did so with explicit written directions, thus flexing their authority and clearly marking their control over the domestic sphere.[12]

Enslaved cooks exhibited incredible skills and techniques

that separated them from the larger labor pool. Cooks were accountable for the production of all daily meals as well as the catering of banquets, presenting a caliber of dining that made Virginia famous for its hospitable nature.[13] This specialized role came with distinctive training, responsibilities, hardships, and perks. Enslaved cooks and their mistresses had a unique relationship that revolved around the production of food, all tangled in the web of power, oppression, violence, and negotiation.[14]

THE VIRGINIA TRADITION

The planter's wife was in charge of the house servants, and she was constantly negotiating her power and control over the meals and labor within her household. However, the success of a meal, especially when guests were being entertained, depended heavily on the cook's ability and in some sense willingness to perform this professional task and put on a "proper" formal dinner. With all the constraints of enslavement in place, some cooks managed to delay special dinners or banquets until they felt ready to perform such a task.[15] These moments of agency were wrapped up in the cook's skill set, which fueled the mistress's respectability in her elite social world. Nonetheless, the cook's role was to produce sophisticated plantation fare, influenced by British and French cuisines and managed by the plantation's mistress. "The matrons of the Old Dominion [had an] enviable reputation for their superb cooking and their delightful housekeeping."[16]

The mistress's reputation was connected to her success as a housewife and was instrumental in portraying herself as the epitome of white womanhood. Even in nineteenth-century housekeeping books this archetype was praised: "Who can find a virtuous woman? For her price is far above rubies. . . . She looketh well to the ways of her household, and eateth not the bread of idleness."[17]

Proper white domesticity was valued above jewels; it was the ultimate goal of many Virginia mistresses.

Virginia's plantations were self-contained social spaces and were sometimes painfully isolated. Many white women were confined to their homes and complained about chronic loneliness. The plantation's distance from the center of town might be more than sixty miles, which created a sense of seclusion based on both locale and the patriarchal desire to protect white womanhood. For some, the planning of social events was their only opportunity for public interaction. Although occasional trips to the market or daily letters connected the mistresses to the happenings of the colony, their world consisted primarily of the household, which acted as a public and highly social venue for Virginia's elites.[18]

This partial seclusion was a common aspect of southern plantation culture.[19] Some women remained inside their domiciles, socializing only with their enslaved domestics. This created among white women a false sense of companionship with their black servants. Jane Edmunds complained about her isolation and the sickly nature of her household. Speaking of her cook Lucy, she wrote, "She is very ill, as are most people in her area, . . . and Harry has everything to do: cook, milk, and wash the clothes." Mrs. Edmunds goes on to mention how she "helps her maids Letia and Betty clean the house."[20] Her life was clearly far from idyllic, and she was no stoic and happy mistress.

Virginia had long been the epitome of domesticity. As early as 1705, noted Englishman Robert Beverly stated, "The kitchen garden don't come any finer than the ones we have in Virginia."[21] Virginia's domestic style was described as a combination of the "thrifty frugality of New England with the less rigid style of Carolina, [and it] has been justly pronounced, by the throngs of admirers who have gathered from all quarters of the Union around the generous boards of her illustrious sons, as the very perfection of domestic art."[22]

The nature of Virginia hospitality was larger than individuals. Elite families would attend church on Sundays and then retire to someone's home for dinner, a barbecue, or a fish fry. Mistresses took turns hosting these Sunday get-togethers. Plantation landscapes were set up to fulfill this function, and white families regularly hosted guests and loved any excuse for a celebration. Even passing strangers, assuming they were white, were treated as welcome guests, and they often brought their enslaved staffs with them. It was common for a neighbor's servant to bring venison or some other delicacy for the master's table.[23]

Mistresses were under tremendous pressure to embody "Virginian domesticity," the precursor of "southern hospitality." Their worth as a wife, the mistress of the house, and a woman was tied to their domestic success, which was directly related to the enslaved cook's skill and the production of desirable food. Mrs. T. J. B. T. Worthington remembered this relationship on her family's plantation:

> Ingleside Plantation outside of Norfolk, was a socially active plantation where the misses was truly "given to hospitality" and constantly entertained family and friends. Family at Ingleside consisted of fifteen people. Neighborhood was very social, had fish fries and picnics. Fourth of July picnics would follow a reading of the constitution and a feast. I well remember how glad we young people were when the celebration was over, we were free to amuse ourselves while the ladies gathered their servant-maids and men and hampers were unpacked and the great feast laid on the rustic table put up for the occasion beneath the trees. And such

a feast! There were home cured hams and great plat-
ters of fried chicken, roasts and joints and vegetables
innumerable; such big pones of "lightened" cornbread
and "beaten biscuit," the like of which only the old
time southern cooks could make. Nobody could beat
our Old Aunt Maria in making biscuit. Wherever a
smaller dish could be set were pickles, jams, tarts and
cakes. The pride of the housewives who complimented
each other's daintiness, doubtless with[out] any mental
reservation. I always noticed that Miss Jane Brown's
pickles and preserves were in great demand and quickly disappeared, for my good auntie was known for the
quality of her good things.[24]

Mrs. Worthington remembered not just the menu but also the
pride her family took in "Old Aunt Maria's" biscuits. Her romanticized recollection of "the old time southern cooks" speaks to
the centrality of food in Virginia's social elite culture, and the
reference to "Aunt Maria" speaks to the presumed familial relationships between white slaveholders and their enslaved cooks.
Domestic pride was so closely linked to the talents of the cook
that the mistress's self-esteem was often based on the doings of
her slaves.

Henry C. Knight, a New England poet, visited Virginia
in 1819 and had a lot to say about his experiences: "Wherever
the Virginians go, a slave or two moves behind as their shadow,
to hold the horses, pull off their boots and pantaloons at bed-
time, and, if cold, to blow up the fire in their bedrooms with their
mouths; bellows being unknown in a slave state." Knight continued: "They sometimes meet, and shoot at a target for a fish-
fry. Fish-fries are held about once in a fortnight, during the fish
season; when twenty or thirty men collect, to regale on whiskey,

and fresh fish, and soft crabs, cooked under a spreading tree, near a running stream, by the slaves." His perspective was from the North, which was not known for its hospitality. Knight was particularly excited about Virginia barbecues: "A more gentile festival is the barbecue, expensive and elegant; where a numerous party of ladies and gentlemen assemble by invitation, or ticket, and feast, and dance, in beautiful decorum, under an artificial arbour. This, as Virginians, living so isolated, are fond of company, produces a course of visiting for weeks afterwards. A Virginian visit is not an afternoon merely; but they go to week it, and to month it, and to summer it."[25]

Knight was struck by the culture of consumption—not only of food but also of whiskey and leisure—which relied on enslaved labor: "As to the diet of Virginians, I may tell you what I observe. Once for all, they are plentiful livers. The first thing in the morning, with many, is the silver goblet of mint-julap. At breakfast, besides their wheaten rolls, they usually have, in their seasons, applt bread, or hominy, with a relish of honey or herring. . . . At dinner which is about three o'clock, whatever other varieties they may have, a tureen of soup, and a chine, jole, or ham of bacon, imbedded with greens about it, are standing dishes."[26] Every one of these items was made by enslaved cooks, highlighting the sophistication of their skills.

Knight's comments were not devoid of racist criticism. The pace at which southerners lived was in stark contrast with that of northerners. This, complicated by white supremacist ideologies, made Knight a cynical critic of his host's staff: "As the kitchens are some rods removed from the dining-hall, at dinner hours you may count long trains of slaves pacing to and fro, with the different viands, for a long time; for, although they have so much help, they are ever in getting a thing done; and thus the dinner is usually comfortably cool before you sit down to it." He continued: "And one need not to be over-fastidious, since, however neat the mistress, good luck if the kitchen is not lined with little half-naked smutchy implings, rolling and clawing about, and listening with impatient delight to slow the revolutions of the spits, and the soft warblings of the caldrons. It is difficult to get over the first prejudices against black servants."[27] He nonetheless benefited from their labor and enjoyed a carefree visit to Virginia.

Mistresses' Reputations

Virginia mistresses managed their households to achieve efficiency. The inner mechanics of a plantation home relied on a full domestic staff working around the clock. Enslaved house maids, waiters, butlers, chamber maids, and cooks all functioned as a larger domestic service network. Enslaved cooks worked closely with the waiters and butlers, as the timing and presentation of food were critical to a meal's success. The mistress often supervised the house cleaning in preparation for dinner guests. At Pine Grove Plantation, the mistress also helped out. Her journal was filled with her daily duties and exposed her obsession with presenting a clean and orderly home. She spent the whole day cleaning and preparing the chamber and dining room for formal dining and rearranging the sideboards, rugs, and so forth. Her dinner guests ate "roasted chicken, boiled potatoes, and then—of soda bread (which the cook succeeds in making very well), milk and preserves."[28] Again, her pride in the cook's food was central to her narrative.

A formal plantation meal required more than a clean house. The butlers and waiters had to set up the dining room with lavish silver, imported European ceramics, candles, and multiple tablecloths, all in preparation for the cook's culinary spread. This cultural standard projected the appropriate self-image for Virginia's plantation elite. The plantation dining room was front stage in the performance of Virginia's domesticity and culinary pride.

There was tremendous pressure on young mistresses to provide this caliber of entertainment, and as a result, the cook inherited the brunt of stress. Plantation women were trying to gain acceptance into elite social circles and had to set the stage with the appropriate props and manners. The mistress at Pine Grove Plantation devoted her entire diary to social planning, mostly concerning food and its role in representing "proper" plantation culture. The diarist notes that although "Molly" had never entertained guests before, she presented an attractive spread of "soda biscuits, two types of preserves, a nice plate of cake, coffee and milk." She goes on to remark that "Mr. Chin and his wife arrived, ate the food and in turn invited [us] to dine at their house." She stresses the importance of this gesture and was obviously elated by the invitation.[29] This momentary exchange illustrates how successful dining acted as an entrée into Virginia's elite culture and that the food served at such occasions needed to be up to par.

The abundant praise for the food served speaks to the fact that it was central to success, yet the absence of critique or complaint begs for an explanation. Perhaps members of the gentry were so wrapped up in courting prestige that they were hesitant to critique a dish. Complimenting the food might have been seen as a marker of social knowledge, a measure of pedigree. It is possible that the newness of this caliber of dining led to a false sense of approval. Perhaps the planters' judgment was not refined enough to critique what they ate. These early generations likely knew *what* beef Bourguignon was but had no idea what it should taste like. Being that these planters and their social equals were not far removed from their unsophisticated ancestors, what kind of culinary comprehension did they really have? There was more at risk in vocally expressing dislike than in singing the praises of a crème brûlée. Expressing one's dislike of a "sophisticated" dish could have been social suicide; one risked being labeled unsophisticated, uncultured, and unworthy of entertainment. While the letters and diaries of plantation mistresses stress the importance of good food, the reality was that most folks lacked the knowledge to properly critique cuisine, yet the function of the supposed measurement acted as a cultural commodity.

The interrelationship between food and domestic success was evident in a popular nineteenth-century kitchen companion: "When the bread rises in the oven, the heart of a housewife rises with it . . . [and] sinks in sympathy with the sinking bread." To prepare for bread-baking "emergencies," the author suggested the following: "I recommend the housekeeper acquire the practice as well as the theory of bread making. In this way, she will be able to give more exact directions to her cook and to more readily detect and rectify any blemish in the bread. Besides, if circumstances should throw her out of a cook for a short time, she is then prepared for the emergency."[30] This direct link between emotion and food speaks to the personal nature of cooking, and the reference to the "emergency" of being without a cook reveals the cook's status in the household and the importance of the mistress maintaining control over her domestic labor and the front stage.

"Carrying the Keys"

Many wealthy southern women were raised with servants, so having enslaved cooks complemented their ideological and physical upbringing. Stepping into the role of mistress was a familiar one, as Virginia elites tended to marry within their social class, making most of these women second-, third-, and fourth-generation mistresses. Their domestic happiness and success were partially tied to their ability to manage servants.[31] Most mistresses were in charge of menu planning, and because they kept many of the ingredients locked up, they were often described as "carrying the keys."[32] This practice was essential to prevent expensive items, such as sugar and spices, from being overused or given away by the cook. Items such as knives and medicinal ingredients were often locked up as a safety measure.

This notion of carrying the keys also referred to the self-assigned role of the mistress, who was in charge of her family and the house servants. Society demanded both ladylike submissiveness and stern leadership from plantation women as they managed their house servants, relying on the master as a last resort. This liminal role provided the mistress with full authority over the domestic sphere, especially the kitchen, which was often separate from the main house and outside of the master's normal dominion. Scholar Linda Parris writes of the mistress, "The tranquility of family, white and black, depended on her ability to settle petty disagreements, cajole, motivate or threaten her servants into working, and all the while maintain an appearance of fragility and ease [to her white socialites]. The failure to be a good mistress, a job involving the duties of both mother and a wife, was a serious breach of gender responsibilities."[33]

Eighteenth-century mistress Elizabeth Foote Washington struggled over her role as a "domestic queen" and wrote:

> It shall be my endeavor not to hurt the feelings of my servants when I am oblig'd to find fault, I will take care not to find fault of one servant before another—but wait with patience [till I have an] opportunity of doing it alone,—if it should be even a day or two before I have one,—by that means I shall teach myself patience & forbearance—& avoid hurting their feelings,—& at the same time raise some ambition in their breast,—for

certainly it must be a pleasing reflection to a servant if they have committed a fault to think no one know it but their mistress.[34]

Perhaps because Mrs. Washington was childless and had suffered repeated miscarriages, she developed a maternal relationship with her domestic slaves. This was not uncommon in Virginia's plantation culture. Because of their physical isolation, many women developed close relationships with their maids and cooks. Their dependence on their enslaved cooks was central to these tangled relationships. The seasoning of dishes, baking of bread, making of preserves, and overall presentation of food were the cook's responsibility, and this created a connection based on the mistress's reliance on and confidence in the cook's skills. Mistresses were not purely motherly toward their cooks, however. They regulated their domestics with strict rules, while trying to be proper southern women.[35]

White southern women also strove to be religious, and their schedules demonstrate their considerable devotion to reading the Bible. Enslaved cooks helped their mistresses maintain this pious lifestyle by making sure the food was served on schedule and removing kitchen-related worries from the mistress's major concerns. According to Anne Frior Scott, "Southern women exerted power within male dominated restrictions," and "a planter's wife was, as a Virginia lady noted, a good housekeeper whether she wanted to be or not."[36]

"Ringing the Dinner Bell"

The image of the leisurely southern woman has reigned in America's collective memory for generations. "Southern women (before 1860) had been the subjects—perhaps the victims—of an image of woman which was at odds with the reality of their lives."[37] The plantation household determined the daily lives of southern white women.[38] The mistress usually arose at 5:00 or 6:00 a.m. to inspect the kitchen.[39] This meant that the cook was already at work on the day's menu. Once the mistress had checked in with the cook and rationed the day's spices, she would turn to other duties such as managing the maids or her children's tutors, writing letters, or reading the Bible.

Mistresses' diaries and notebooks expose their diverse responsibilities within the household. They often wore many hats, depending on their households' needs. Maria Nelson of Westover Plantation kept a schoolbook that contained recipes for huckleberry cake, spiced grapes, dressings, chocolate filling, orange cake, brownies delight cake, wafers, delicious orange dessert, caramel filling, custard filling, cream puffs, pies, cakes, doughnuts, fillings, and waffles, all interspersed with lessons on history, philosophy, and arithmetic.[40] The predominance of sweet recipes suggests that she oversaw the cooks' dessert making, since the mistresses usually locked up the sugar.

While the mistress was occupied managing the household, the cook was busy preparing an average of four meals a day: breakfast, dinner, tea, and supper.[41] Many plantations had dinner bells that announced when meals were served, and the duty of ringing the bell was shared with the cook and sometimes the wait staff. Phillip Fithian, the Carter family tutor, remembered this tradition: "Ms. Carter has a large good bell of upwards of 60 lbs which may be heard some miles, & this is always rung at meal times."[42] Breakfast was set out at daybreak and was available until midmorning, as many of the folks living at the plantation had different morning schedules. The cook prepared biscuits, breads, meats, and porridge, along with preserves, coffee, and tea. Some of the James River plantations served oysters at every meal, as they were fresh and accessible. Fithian noted the dining schedule at Virginia's Nomini Hall Plantation: "Half after eight the bell rings for breakfast . . . breakfast till 9:30, dinner bell at commonly 2:30, often 3 but never before 2! After dinner is over, which in common if we have no company, is about half after three . . . supper is 8:30 or at 9."[43] This schedule outlines the cook's routine, beginning at daybreak and ending well after nightfall.

Occasionally the mistress got her hands in the flour and actually cooked—sometimes alongside the cook, but more likely in his or her absence. In June 1823 an unnamed mistress wrote, "Last Monday dear Caroline was married . . . yesterday we gave them a large dinner party. I had fatigued myself so much making a dessert over the fire that when the hour came that was to call my guests to dinner I was obliged to take Seidlitz powders and bind my head with poplar leaves."[44] This brief stint in the kitchen fatigued the mistress so much that she required medicinal treatment. Cooking just one dish was more than she could handle, indicating the intensity of the schedules of enslaved cooks, who served four meals every day.

Plantation dinners were the pulse of Virginia's domestic pride and reputation. Fithian fondly remembered these grand suppers: "We were rung into supper. The room looked luminous and splendid; four very large candles burning on the table where we supp'd, three others in different parts of the room: a gay, sociable assembly & four well instructed waiters!"[45] Fellow Virginian Helen Coles also described these meals: "We sat down to dinner drest in our best, and looking as though we had never thought of anything more pleasant than to simply taste the various delicacies placed before us—such a dinner was customarily served by placing a variety of dishes on the table, which was later cleared for the dessert course."[46] Coles commented:

> We were entertained in a most sumptuous fashion . . .
> the table was spread with double table cloths and the

first course consisted of beef, mutton, oysters, soup, etc. The first cloth was removed with these viands, and the clean one below covered with pies, puddings, tarts, jellies, whips, floating island, sweetmeats, etc. and after these we came to the plain mahogany table. Clean glasses were brought on and a lighter kind of wine with fruit, raisins and almonds . . . a typical first course would include a large standing cold ham wrapped in a linen napkin at the top of the table balanced by a hot saddle of mutton, leg of lamb, roast beef, turkey or goose at the bottom of the table . . . the centerpiece might be a mock turtle, a huge meat pie, a haunch of venison, or a made dish, a complicated composition of meat, sauced and garnished with such ingredients as eels, chicken livers, mushrooms, oysters and coxcombs.[47]

These culinary spreads were influenced by both British and French culture. Elite Virginians, who were mostly of English descent, had their own traditions, while the idea of French food carried significant cultural currency. However, black cooks undoubtedly introduced West African foodways to these to European styles, creating a distinct southern cuisine. The rise of French cuisine allowed mistresses to flaunt their culinary sophistication by including a variety of sauces and sides rather than a simple roasted meat.[48] This elevated them from the embarrassment of medieval cooking into the elite world of fine cuisine. Preparing an overly technical and delicate menu required particular skills, and enslaved cooks stepped up and proved themselves fully capable of executing fine culinary fare. French cooking required time, which was something mistresses were unwilling to give.

Eating in the French fashion meant consuming sauces and condiments that made each dish superbly delicious. In addition,

"Sugar from the West Indies gave rise to desserts. Upper-class Anglo-Americans thought French cuisine was superior to their own."[49] This French influence began in the eighteenth century and became part of Virginia cuisine by the 1800s. Eating in the French fashion also meant serving a large variety of food but eating only some of it. This tradition marked a transition from eating for sustenance to eating as a performance of elite "cultured" ways. It also illustrated a connection between wealth and waste. The food, as such, became an essential "prop" within Virginia's plantation society and its overt style of conspicuous consumption. Knight described a typical Virginia supper:

> As the Virginians expend all their strength upon dinner, their supper is a mere ceremony. They have not, as we have, a table, and toast, and pies, and cake; but, at about dusk, is sent around to each one, as he sits in the hall, or under the piazza, a cup of coffee, or tea, or both. Then follows a round plate of biscuits on a tray, hot, and about as large as a small letter-wafer; and perhaps a Virginian may sip a whole cup, and nibble a half or even a whole biscuit; but as frequently neither. Some epicures after this apology, have a flesh or crawfish supper, at ten o'clock, to sleep on, and to accommodate them with the fashionable dyspepsy.[50]

Later in the 1850s, Frederick Olmsted commented on the Virginia dining scene:

> A stout woman acted as head waitress, employing two handsome little mulatto boys as her aids in communicating with the kitchen, from which relays of hot corn-bread, of an excellence quite new to me, were at

frequent intervals. There was no other bread, and but one vegetable served—sweet potato, roasted in ashes, and this, I thought, was the best sweet potato, also, that I had ever eaten; but there were four preparations of swine's flesh, besides fried fowls, fried eggs, cold roast turkey, and opossum, cooked, I know not how, but it somewhat resembled baked sucking-pig. The only beverages on the table were milk and whiskey. . . . The house-servants were neatly dressed, but the field-hands wore very coarse and ragged garments.[51]

Virginia hospitality was an all-service machine, relying on a network of enslaved laborers to welcome guests. Guests at Shirley Plantation were each given an individual servant to aid them during their stay. A typical day's eating schedule began with an 8:00 a.m. breakfast consisting of coffee, tea, hot breads, and ham served on a bare table. By 1:00 p.m. the guests would convene—the men drinking and the women socializing; then dinner was served at 3:00. The dining table had layers of tablecloths, each of which was removed by the waiters after each course. They served the food in the French style. For the first course there were several meats, sauces, and sides such as mutton, duck, oysters, greens, sweet potatoes, and hominy. The second course consisted of freshly baked pastries, tarts, ice creams, brandied fruit, and preserves. The meal ended with wine, nuts, and dried fruit. The women often left after the last course, leaving the men to drink and socialize.[52]

Special Occasions: Balls and Banquets

In addition to everyday fare, Virginia was known for its lavish social events. The classic image of the plantation social scene was a room full of jewel-adorned white women wearing vibrant silk dresses, lace, bonnets, and petticoats, waiting for handsome bachelors to arrive in horse and buggy to find their future wives. There would be ballroom dancing and small symphonies, as well as tables filled with silver, crystal, and an abundance of food and spirits. This image of plantation culture came from the numerous formal events put on by Virginia's mistresses during the eighteenth and nineteenth centuries.

Plantation balls were planned well in advance and were advertised accordingly. It was common for the mistresses to post notices of these events, as they were responsible for the planning and execution of such occasions. As seen in the *Virginia Gazette*, these notices became more detailed as the date of the event drew closer. For example, the first advertisement for a Williamsburg ball read: "Mrs. Degraffendriedt gives notice that she intends to have a Ball at her house on Tuesday November 1st, and an assembly the next day."[53] Two weeks later, the advertisement stated: "This is to inform Gentlemen and Ladies that Mrs. Degraffendriedt designs to have a Ball at her house, on Tuesday the first of November next, and a Collation, for the Entertainment of those who are pleased to favor her with their company, for which tickets will be delivered at her House at Five Shillings each. . . . And the next day she designs to have an assembly for which Tickets will be delivered at her House, at Half a Pistole each."[54] The fact that tickets were being sold for this event ensured that the guest list would be plump with well-off Virginians and that the plantation's air of sophistication would be maintained. The updated version of the advertisement also spoke to the fact that it was a designated space for both men and women—a courting zone—where elites could mingle while maintaining the pretensions of plantation sophistication. This tradition complicated the idea of white womanhood and showed the public nature of women's role in elite culture.

These occasions were important social outlets and the perfect stage for the exhibition of domestic crafts. Banquet tables were often decorated with ribbons and multiple tablecloths. "The centerpiece was an elaborate 'temple of love' made of spun sugar, surely originating from the labor of enslaved Africans in the West Indies. In the 19th century, such 'temples' were very popular as wedding table decorations."[55] Punch bowls were filled with homemade fruit brandy; tables were laden with delightful sugary tarts, candies, and sweets.[56] Plantations took turns hosting these parties, which allowed the mistresses to showcase their homes, their organizational skills, and their ability to create European-inspired cuisine, albeit by their enslaved cooks.

These parties, though grand and fancy, were not always as romantic as one might think. Despite the ball gowns and the silver, the roughness of Virginia's rural nature often shined through. A European visitor wrote in 1780, "Another peculiarity of this country is the absence of napkins, even in the homes of the wealthy. Napkins as a whole are never used and one has to wipe one's mouth on the table cloth, which in consequence suffers in appearance."[57] The image of a silk-dressed maiden leaning down to wipe her mouth on the tablecloth contradicts the popular notion of elite manners. However, this peculiarity existed within Virginia's isolated plantation community.

These special occasions were not only important social outlets; they were also vital to familial success. These events were the pinnacle of plantation life and provided a much-needed venue for social interaction among whites. It was at these balls that men and women found their future spouses and families secured elite and wealthy heirs. In January 1832 George Blow wrote a letter to John Y. Mason, bragging about his daughter's invitation to a splendid ball at Belfield Plantation.[58] The successful ball boasted a long guest list that provided a broad but elite source of eligible bachelors and bachelorettes.

Domestic pride and performance were directly connected with marital success and moral worth. This relationship was outlined in a Virginia housekeeping book:

> If she shall thus make her tasks lighter and home-life sweeter; if she shall succeed in contributing something to the health of American children by instructing their mothers in the art of preparing light and wholesome and palatable food; *if she above all, shall succeed in making American Homes more attractive to American husbands, and spare them a resort to hotels and saloons for those simple luxuries which their wives know how not to provide;* if she shall thus add to the comfort, to the health and happy contentment of these, she will have proved in some measure a public benefactor, and will feel amply repaid for all the labor her work has cost.[59]

This ideology reigned in nineteenth-century Virginia and fueled the need for "good house help," for without it, one's marriage was doomed and one's moral worth was at risk. Because food was a critical factor in the popularity of a plantation's event, enslaved cooks were vital contributors to their mistresses' domestic pride, which included the achievement of ideal domesticity, cultural production, and respectability. In addition, because these formal balls were designated as "courting spaces," the cooks' labor was connected to the success of future marriages, the spawning of familial heirs, and the maintenance of Virginia's elite plantation pedigree.

The critical role of food and meals also expanded into men's social lives. Plantation dinners, though planned by the mistress and produced by the cook, were essential to planters' professional success. Virginia's plantation dining rooms provided additional space for men to meet, eat, and discuss formal business matters with other planters, doctors, lawyers, and government officials. Nineteenth-century planter Dr. Richard Eppes noted that he "held formal meetings during dinner" and used the time to network with other influential men.[60] Meals and food were imperative to the overall accomplishments of Virginia's plantation households.

Buying Success: The Cook as Commodity

Since food was such a critical part of a plantation's operation and success, enslaved cooks were highly valued and sought after. For a mistress to have a proper home, she needed to have a skilled cook, whether obtained through inheritance or purchase. Virginia newspapers were filled with notices advertising the sale of everything from land to enslaved blacks. Among thousands of eighteenth-century ads, cooks were clearly a highly valued commodity. For example, the March 8, 1770, issue of the *Virginia Gazette* advertised a sale at the Amelia courthouse of "ABOUT 20 very likely *Virginia* born SLAVES, chiefly men and women, . . . and one of them a very good cook."[61] Another ad read, "I have for sale a negro woman that is generally thought of by those that know her an exceeding good COOK," and "TEN likely Virginia born NEGROES, all under 20 years of age but one, which is about 38, a good cook, and as handy a wench as any in the colony."[62] This sort of promoted value was rampant and spoke to a particular audience—those who wanted a skilled cook to enhance their household's status and reputation. Age was another indication of a cook's level of worth, in that kitchen skills accumulated and grew over time. While field hands might get weaker with age, a cook's talent only increased.

Planters maintained a goal of self-sufficiency, and the plantation system of meal preparation and production fit this mode perfectly and was central to the development of Virginia's hospitable nature. Eighteenth-century bourgeois rhetoric of domesticity became ingrained in nineteenth-century cultural norms.[63] Plantation mistresses desired, managed, and promoted their domestic success and relied on their cooks to achieve this caliber of domestic production. While the plantation acted as a stage for the performance of domesticity, the main players—the cooks, the domestic servants, and the mistresses—alternated between two stages and acted differently, depending on which stage they were on. The main house—its ballroom, hall, parlor, and dining room—constituted the front stage, the formal space for social functions; this was where guests were entertained and proper etiquette was demanded. The actors on this stage, in the classic southern manner, were polite, polished players. When the butler or the cook announced, "Mistis, dinner is served," they were using that front-stage persona.[64] However, their performance changed drastically when dinner was over, the guests went home, and the curtain closed on the front stage.

AFRICA ON THE TABLE

The history of African foodways in America traditionally existed only in the minds of the cooks. Until the nineteenth century, there was no written record. The oral tradition was central in preserving the rich cultures of enslaved Africans, especially during the slave trade. Just as geographic locations yielded specific crops, individuals from different places brought their own cooking styles and techniques. This pragmatic assumption is the foundation of this section.

The scarcity of written records describing early African influences on American food has forced scholars to take an interdisciplinary approach. Travelers' accounts, diaries, letters, and receipt books yield some information, but the absence of specificities with regard to cuisine and ingredients leads one to look elsewhere for supplementation, including written records, oral histories, archaeological data, and architectural sources. It is through these diverse perspectives that one can triangulate the information and create a multidimensional narrative that unveils the influences of West African foodways in Virginia and throughout the Atlantic world.

Many of the early written records focused on European-inspired menus and excluded the African influence on ingredients and recipes. By the nineteenth century, white mistresses were recording such recipes in cookbooks, including many African-influenced dishes. By 1824, Virginia housewife Mary Randolph had chronicled recipes such as ochre (okra) and tomatoes, gumbo, and this recipe for pepper pot: "Boil two or three pounds of tripe, cut it in pieces, and put it on the fire with a knuckle of veal, and a sufficient quantity of water; part of a pod of pepper, a little spice, sweet herbs according to your taste, salt, and some dumplins; stew it till tender, and thicken the gravy with butter and flour."[65]

Such traditional African dishes were cooked in the homes of planters as well as in the slaves' field quarters. Their popularity is proved by their inclusion in receipt books. Once a recipe makes its way into a cookbook, it has passed a cultural test. It becomes more than a memory; it is a reminder that must be cooked and eaten again. The appearance of these West African dishes in published cookbooks indicates the acceptance of African food and its importance as a signifier of socioeconomic class, national identity, and pride. Literate housewives read these recipes and duplicated them in the ultimate performance of white womanhood—mimicking plantation fare that was clearly a mixture of European and African food. The recipes that made their way into published works were certainly not the only dishes cooked; rather, they were the favorite dishes. Countless other African dishes were cooked, served, and eaten by colonists throughout the centuries. Ingredients and recipes tell the history of enslaved cooks from their ancestral homes in West Africa, through the Middle Passage, and into Anglo kitchens, where their talents became irreplaceable.[66]

It is challenging to tease out the precise influences of West African foodways in colonial Virginia. Colonists were transferring a plethora of foodstuffs, some of which were West African in origin and quickly became part of Virginian and Atlantic cuisine. What culinary historian James C. McCain calls the "Atlantic circulation," also known as the "Columbian trade," drastically transformed global markets, which had previously been semibound to land.[67] Black-eyed peas, okra, millet, and yams are some of the ingredients that directly transformed the new colonies' crops and dinner tables. However, the essence of culinary influence is found not simply in these key ingredients but rather in the techniques of African cooks, whose memories, creativity, and effort transformed crops into cuisine. Although many different factors influenced the flavor of plantation cuisine, the Igbo's use of okra is one of the most prominent legacies in southern foodways.[68] It was used as a thickening agent, and enslaved cooks relied on this ingredient, which probably became a good substitute for a roux. Presumably enslaved cooks had knowledge, either firsthand or passed down, of how to make certain foods from their homeland. For example, palm wine was a common staple in many parts of West Africa, as were fried foods and stews. Their organic culinary knowledge was easily transferable to the elite plantation culture.[69]

Foodways of the African diaspora are complicated and diverse, having been influenced by enslavement, forced labor, and the constant need to adapt to new surroundings. Foodways exemplify the cultural importance of food as a way to maintain connections to one's ancestors and to a land and people left behind. Instead of simply looking at the edible influences brought by enslaved Africans, it is important to consider the transformation from the perspective of the diverse interfaces that occurred during colonization. For example, a traditional foodways approach would simply trace how African flavors altered traditional colonial fare. Although this approach shows the significance of African foodways, it takes the perspective of the colonists and avoids a holistic understanding of how adaptation and agency affected cuisine and dining as a whole, as well as its intersections with race, class, and gender dynamics. Forced interactions created a complicated web of cultural, economic, and regional differences in food preparation, consumption, and culture. It is not the food that makes a cuisine; rather, it is the cook that creates and sustains it. This is the narrative of crop and hand, technique and utensil, memory and adaptation; it is the story of the transformation of dining in the English-speaking Atlantic world that began in West Africa and carried into colonial Virginia plantations.

It is hard to decipher the enslaved diet without archaeological evidence, and the function of the kitchen as a space for cultural reproduction makes it an essential focal point for research on foodways. Examining the discarded animal bones from the kitchen quarters' trash pits helps unveil the diet and culinary techniques of enslaved cooks. Faunal remains are invaluable in demonstrating that enslaved African Americans supplemented their diets with food from their own gardens, wild animals caught on their own time, and food from the marketplace.

Archaeologist Maria Franklin argues that enslaved African Americans in Virginia ate cuts of meat that the planters did not want. In her work at Rich Neck Plantation in Williamsburg, Franklin found that contemporary notions of "good" and "bad" cuts of meat were reversed in colonial Virginia. She states, "What we today would consider the cheapest, least desirable portions of an animal were consumed eagerly on a regular basis by even elite slave owning whites."[70] Thus, the archaeological evidence from slave quarters shows that enslaved African Americans consumed what we now consider higher-quality cuts of meat, supplemented with wild animals and fish.

Enslaved plantation cooks single-handedly transformed American food and gave birth to southern cuisine. The West African ingredients and cooking techniques passed down through generations melded with European methods and ingredients and allowed cooks to create distinct menus. These contributions are undeniable, yet their cultural roots are often ignored or forgotten.

IN MEMORY

Kitchen Ghosts

While slavery ended more than 150 years ago, its legacy permeates our social, cognitive, and material worlds. The depth and breadth of its legacy cover almost every aspect of our society, and the lingering ideological memory of enslaved cooks is entrenched in American grocery and culinary trends. Boxes of Aunt Jemima pancake mix and Uncle Ben's rice fill our grocers' shelves, using the images of enslaved cooks to authenticate these products. This mythical cook is so ingrained in American culture and consciousness that we have neglected to interrogate this widely accepted idea. This book redefines the mythical "slave cook" and uncovers the rich and complex history of these individuals and their role in plantation culture. Plantation tours have a responsibility to present ethical and holistic narratives formed by recent scholarship, oral histories, and archaeological evidence. Historical and archaeological data are critical in reinforming contemporary mythical ideas about enslaved cooks and their kitchens and reshaping their legacy in America's cultural history.

The lasting images of enslaved cooks flood flea markets, antique stores, and online auctions. These objects, often in the form of kitchenware, remind us of the Old South, where racist ideologies took tangible form. While black Americana continues to re-inforce ideas about black servitude and white privilege, it also acts as a medium for redefinition and has an immense ability to evoke reactions from us all.

Alongside the trend of grocery product advertising, black Americana material culture developed and gained popularity. Statues, kitchenware, and countless random items used the images of black-faced cooks to reinforce the racist and sexist memory of enslaved cooks. These material manifestations laid such a solid foundation in American memory that, until recently, even scholars had not delved into this vat of institutionalized racism and misrepresentation. These images functioned in many ways. They were specifically targeted toward white Americans' fear of integration. Black Americana led white folks to believe that the old days were still in reach and that the black body, though free, was still controlled by white power. Having the *image* of a black cook in one's kitchen meant that the "ease" of black servitude was carried over, without having an *actual* black body inside one's home. This conflicting mentality directly reflects plantation settings, where the black body was put to work, but at a proper distance.

Americans are so used to the idea of black cooks that the latter's history has been marginalized. During my research for this book, scholars in other fields expressed doubt that there was anything new to bring to the table. But the slave cook as a white-washed Uncle Tom or mammy is far from reality. Scholarship on foodways has successfully depicted how enslaved cooks manipulated food and created a creolized cuisine. This book, in conjunction with historical research on foodways, enslavement, and plantation history, pulls the individual voices from the records. The written record reveals the whole stage—front, back, and in between—and describes a vibrant social space within the dregs of slavery and the excruciating labor demands. The archaeology unearths the tangible ways these cooks actively remembered their past, helped themselves and others survive the horrors of chattel slavery, and continued to own their identities as African people. They, unlike the field hands, were part of the white landscape and had to participate in the performance of white domesticity. In all this, they were more complex than the myth suggests. If, in fact, Aunt Jemima pancakes were served with a side of contempt, or Rastus's Cream of Wheat came with a Sankofa-shaped spoon, or, even better, Uncle Ben's rice contained trace amounts of poison, we would be closer to reality.

For antique collectors, black Americana is a moneymaker. Whether such objects engender fascination, obsession, or pure disdain, consumers buy them as fast as they are offered. On e-Bay, it is rare for any item of black Americana to go without a bid, and the most popular ones depict either Aunt Jemima or some other generic black cook. Stoneycreek Candle Company has taken advantage of the market for black Americana, mass-producing soy candles in old tin cans with newly painted slave-cook imagery. These images reinforce ideas about African American labor and its place in American homes.

Similarly, the legacy of racialized domestic labor can be seen throughout elite Virginia institutions, including its universities and colleges. Private homes still rely on majority-black staffs to cater to and serve majority-white guests. I witnessed an event where the all-black kitchen staff, waiters, maids, and cook were thanked at the end of the meal—an awkward ritual harking back to the nineteenth century. Similarly, black guests are often presumed to be the "help" by white guests, creating an awkward and unwelcoming atmosphere. On one occasion, the bizarreness increased when I was told that the "help" lived on the plantation— right where the slave quarters had once stood. The elite's kitchens are still highly racialized, especially given the influx of Latin immigrants and the persistent population of working-class African Americans. Having personally cooked in private homes and dined at present-day plantations and universities, it is very clear to me that the complex legacy of plantation cooking and racialized labor remains active.

MYTH, GENDER, AND AMERICAN MEMORY

Booker T. Washington wrote in his 1915 classic *Up from Slavery:* "When a Negro girl learns to cook, to wash dishes, to sew, to write a book, or a Negro boy learns to groom horses, or to grow sweet potatoes, or to produce butter, or to build a house, or to be able to practice medicine—they will be rewarded regardless of race or colour."[1] By the early twentieth century, gender constructions were directly connected with labor roles; specifically, women were identified as cooks. This relationship was popularized by the fictional character of Aunt Jemima, but it had little basis in reality.

In the early eighteenth century men were believed to be better cooks and were highly sought after. This trend can be seen in advertisements in the *Virginia Gazette*. One that appeared in November 1778 stated: "WANTED: John Parke Custis/Williamsburg I will give a generous ready money price for a good COOK. A man would be preferred."[2] Popular eighteenth-century thought connected masculinity with the ability to withstand the heat and the physical labor involved in kitchen work. Two other ads showcased the kitchen skills of the men for sale: "An exceeding likely and capable young NEGRO FELLOW who understands House Work . . . and is a tolerable good Cook,[3] and "an exceeding likely young negro man, who is a very good house servant, and is a tolerable good cook. If purchaser is not perfectly satisfied with him after month's trial, he may return him if in health."[4] In addition, William Plume of Williamsburg wrote, "I would exchange a negro man, who is a good house servant and cook, and by profession a biscuit baker."[5] This demonstrates the professionalism of some enslaved cooks and the respect their skills brought them. A cook who could produce all types of foods was a valuable commodity, as indicated in this 1776 ad: "A GOOD negro COOK, who is a healthy fellow under 40 years of age, can roast and broil very well, and understands made dishes, with baking of bread and pickling."[6] This enslaved man had obviously been trained to reproduce European fare.

Masculinity and blackness carried a variable identity that transformed as the years progressed. While it was common to have an enslaved man as a plantation cook in the eighteenth century, by the nineteenth century, women had become more popular in the kitchen. The "feminization" of the domestic sphere was a gradual transition as more women were sold into slavery and made their way into plantation kitchens. One can also assume that with the increase and formalization of elite white women as mistresses, the power dynamic between race and gender shifted. As more white women became part of the household and assumed greater domestic responsibility and control, there were fewer male cooks. This might have been due to white fear of the black male slave and the desire to "protect" white womanhood. Or it could be attributable to both the expansion of specialized plantation labor, such as blacksmithing and other male-dominated trades that took men out of the kitchen, and the overall increase of enslaved women in the South.

Enslaved women were also considered more valuable due to their childbearing abilities. Black women were viewed as both productive and reproductive as they labored alongside men and bore children to replenish the labor pool. Racial discrimination was compounded by sexual prejudice, and enslaved women were victims of sexual, emotional, and physical abuse. There was a dual caste system based on race and sex, and plantations were a microcosm of this order. Two forms of domination overlapped: traditional notions of womanhood and the profit-plantation economy. The "colonial household industry" relied on enslaved folks to carry out domesticity through their labor, skills, and presence. The labor of enslaved women was used to keep crops up, enlarge the workforce, and sustain the plantation household.[7]

Approaching the study of enslaved cooks from multiple angles allows one to examine many facets of their lives. The moments and materials captured in time can reveal only so much, but the cumulation of these elements can shed light on their struggles, their agency, and their daily activities. It is essential to redefine the enslaved cook as skilled, literate, intelligent, and somewhat powerful within the limits of his or her position. They used their talents to gain power and take control of their social and physical environments for themselves and their families. Enslaved cooks were vital to the success of their white mistresses and plantation social functions. They were also central to other slaves' ability to persevere by providing access to alternative space. The myth of the whitewashed cook considers only the front-stage persona; a look back stage shows that enslaved cooks retained their African heritage and their religious and cultural roots, despite being placed in the white landscape.

We must remember not just the pain of slavery or the strange legacy of Aunt Jemima or Uncle Rastus but also the dignity of enslaved cooks, the pride they took in their food, and their ability to negotiate their labor and living conditions for themselves and their loved ones within the kitchen walls.

Plantation Tourism

Anyone who has visited a plantation museum can testify that there are many "political" moments during these tours. Whether this involves the mention of Sally Hemmings at just the right time or the docents' attempts to skirt issues related to slavery by highlighting the "good times" of the plantation, these moments hinder an honest representation of plantation life. One particular tactic is to focus on the aesthetics of the plantation, and particularly the dining room, where tales of the mistress entertaining her guests take front stage. Some docents tell visitors that the mistress cooked the food or even washed the fine china after dinner.[8] These discussions of labor are unacceptable, as they fail to address the reasons why the mistress may have washed her own china (to ensure that it was not broken); nor do they acknowledge the staff of enslaved domestics that cooked for, cleaned up after, and served the white family.

Another political ploy involves the "whistling walkway," such as the one at Berkeley Plantation in Charles City County, which displays signage to mark this renowned path (see figure 7). The underground passage was dug between the external kitchen and the mansion cellar, which eventually led to the formal dining room via a narrow flight of stairs built between the walls. The story goes that the mistress required the enslaved cook or waitperson to whistle while carrying the food to the main house to ensure that he or she did not eat it. This bizarre ritual makes no sense as it is described by the plantation tour guide. This interpretation assumes that the cook had not touched the food while preparing it or had avoided tasting it in the process. It ignores the fact that black labor was intimately involved in creating and producing meals and presumes that the cook or waiter was untrustworthy and in need of surveillance. In addition, the demand for whistling implies a particular level of forced performance. Having the black servant whistle or sing as the food was brought inside could be interpreted as a form of entertainment for the white family and guests. Alternatively, it could have warned whites of

Figure 7. Sign for the whistling walkway at Berkeley Plantation in Charles City County. (Author's collection)

the approach of an enslaved person, signaling them to halt their conversation or certain improper behaviors. Either way, these whistling walkways acted as a venue for black performance and an architectural manifestation of the social control of enslaved spaces.

Such absurd tales function to ease white tourists' feelings about slavery and the personal intimacy between blacks and whites, while perpetuating stereotypes of the bad character and dishonesty of African Americans. During the Jim Crow era, many white southerners reimagined their relationship to blacks as one of separation and distance. Many of the distorted notions we have about the past come from this reimagining of social history during the era of segregation. Once slavery was abolished, white southerners successfully enforced a series of laws that physically separated blacks and whites in public spaces. After 246 years of living in close proximity to one another, fearful whites decided to recalibrate the social structure to ignore hundreds of years of co-existence. Fearful whites reimagined and rewrote the past to fit a narrative that supported Jim Crow culture. Just as the nineteenth-century whistling walkways and secret passageways were built to hide black bodies from white guests, tour guides' twisted versions of reality wrapped in twentieth-century folklore exist to redefine history and remove the enslaved black body from the intimacy that occurred during food production.

The legacies of plantation kitchens and racialized labor are substantial. The cultural landscapes of Virginia gave birth to a formalized culture of hospitality that spread throughout the American South. This regional reputation still prevails. Enslaved cooks were at the core of this evolution, and their kitchens were the manifestation of these ideological trends. The birth of "other-ness" and racial landscapes also grew alongside and in response to these notions and existed throughout the twentieth century and into the twenty-first.

Every year, thousands of tourists flock to Virginia to "step back in time" by visiting Colonial Williamsburg, the James River Plantation, or similar venues. Plantation kitchens remain a per-manent fixture in the tourist landscape, while most slave cabins and quarters were demolished long ago. Colonial Williamsburg rents out its kitchens at a higher price than its hotel rooms, of-fering an "authentic experience." It does not, however, rent slave quarters, as that would be too controversial. This decision to sell only the kitchen as a "safe space" for tourists speaks to the kitch-en's position not only in history but also in our chosen memo-ries. Somehow, kitchens have become one of the only acceptable facets in the interpretation and commoditization of enslavement. This speaks to the importance of the kitchen and the cook in the legacy of public historical memory. Although tours may fail to present enslaved cooks in a realistic and respectful manner, the shadows of these cooks stand strong in the buildings they once called home.

The Emancipation of Emmanuel Jones

Emmanuel Jones rose early to the sound of roosters crowing to cook breakfast for his master. He lived in the kitchen at Flowerdew Hundred Plantation, adjacent to the big house and within walking distance of the field quarters. The smell of the James River and the nearby trash deposits often carried into the kitchen and mixed with the scents of his culinary creations. He was proud of his cooking skills and was known on the plantation as "the little Black magician" because "his biscuits were so good, it was like magic." His mother Keziah was the plantation milkmaid; his father Emmanuel Jones Sr. lived on the property as well. Born in the 1840s, Emmanuel Jr. spent the first twenty-plus years of his life enslaved by the Wilcox family, owners of Flowerdew Hundred Plantation in Prince George County, Virginia.

On any given day, Emmanuel and his family would throw their garbage into the outdoor trash pit, a common practice at the time. This pit was located on the side of the kitchen that faced the field quarters, out of view of the main house. Cooking for the Wilcoxes and his own family created a significant amount of garbage—animal remains, broken dishes, bottles, and so forth. The Joneses also dug root cellars inside the kitchen, under the floors, to keep the root vegetables dry and cool, as well as to hide their valuables. More than a hundred years later, some of these items remained in place, offering material testimony to the private world of an enslaved cook. Little did Mr. Jones know that one day his garbage and his valuables would tell his story, and that his story would change the way we think of the black folks who worked in the big house.

Established in 1619, Flowerdew Hundred is one of Virginia's oldest plantations. This 1,000-acre plantation was home to many early white settlers, as well as to some of the first Africans brought through Jamestown in 1619. It is believed that the first African American was born on this land shortly after its founding. This plantation witnessed many significant historical moments and has an unmatched archaeological record. In 1804 John V. Wilcox purchased the land for himself and his new wife, Susanna Peachy Poythress. Following local tradition, the Wilcoxes erected an external kitchen for the cook just south of the main house and north of the slave quarters. By 1830, the Wilcox family had created a fully developed plantation community.[9] The kitchen was constructed on a brick pier foundation and had a raised plank floor, glass windows, and two fireplace hearths, one on each side of the dwelling.

Keziah and her family remained on the plantation during the Civil War. Emmanuel Jr. continued to live on the plantation and cook for the Wilcoxes long after obtaining his freedom. He eventually left Flowerdew Hundred in the late nineteenth century and moved to Petersburg, Virginia, where he bought a plot of land, raised a family, and worked as a cook until the day he died on August 21, 1917. The Flowerdew kitchen was occupied by members of the Jones family until they moved, at which point it was turned into a workshop-garage, as depicted in a 1930s photograph.

This specific site, like many of those dug in the 1980s and earlier, was excavated and recorded without extensive knowledge of African diaspora traditions. Focusing a twenty-first-century lens on the Wilcox kitchen reveals a number of things that were unknown to the original archaeologists. The kitchen had significant artifact deposits in and around the hearth. A small amethyst crystal was located in the subfloor pit of the northeast hearth. The use of such crystals in a form of religious "root work" began in many parts of West Africa and survived in the Americas.[10] The location is congruent with evidence that these caches were intentionally placed, usually in the northeast section of a dwelling space. In addition to this gem, oyster shells were found in the same location, symbolizing the color white and the world of the ancestors. Both are evidence of traditional West African religion, and such items were historically used in the practice of hoodoo. Many ethnic groups believed that at death their souls traveled back through the ocean into the ancestral land, where all was white. The discovery of such shells, though seemingly unimportant to the untrained eye, can shed light on the cognitive spiritual world of enslaved African cooks and, specifically, the hidden dimensions of the Joneses' religious practices.

The Role of Archaeology and History

When these clues buried deep in the earth are excavated, they provide tremendous insight into the lives of the enslaved. Historical archaeology is essential to understanding the history of those who could not speak for themselves. Enslaved folks were often illiterate, and after Nat Turner's 1831 rebellion, it became illegal for them to learn to read or write. Often, their garbage is the only means we have to understand the details of their daily lives. Kitchen garbage is generally a complicated mix of both black and white trash, highlighting the intimate intersection between these two separate yet highly integrated worlds. Plates that graced the tables of elite whites might be found crushed alongside hand-me-down cups from the kitchen quarters. These material remnants provide rich evidence of their users' lives.

Historians and archaeologists have a responsibility to provide testimony on behalf of the ancestors. This is a sensitive and challenging task. The archaeology of plantation kitchens allows a path for public engagement that archival research does not. The descendants of the enslaved can recognize these material items and shed light on their meanings. African diaspora culture is strong, rich, and diverse, and it has survived in ways not clearly seen by most Americans. So much of America is culturally African, and food is only a portion of this legacy.

Archaeological investigations of kitchens can reveal information about the complex social space in which enslaved cooks lived and worked; it can expose the liminal nature of their lives, in the sense that they existed between two worlds. Field quarters and mansion homes have been thoroughly examined, but kitchens have usually been assigned to one or the other, rather than being treated as separate and distinct spaces. Eighteenth-century plantation culture was diverse, and the archaeology of kitchens exemplifies that historical moment and suggests that African and European material culture coexisted in the kitchen. While the voices of eighteenth-century enslaved Africans were missing from the larger historical record, their material culture speaks loudly on their behalf. As the nineteenth century approached and American slavery matured, the written record captured more enslaved voices, while the material culture became more covert and creolized. Archaeology uncovers how these cooks remembered their past and preserved their identity.

As scholars move forward and learn more about the experiences of the enslaved, they must continue to engage with descendant communities. This work is a testament to more than 150 years of miseducation and the need to reevaluate what has been taken for granted. Archaeologists will continue to excavate sites related to slavery and reveal more stories through artifacts. For instance, the kitchen at Dixon Plantation held an assortment of modified cowrie shells, African glass beads, and a pierced English coin. This array of materials is representative of enslaved Africans' ability to hold on to some of their material goods during the horrors of their transatlantic voyage. The coin, though not African, was modified in an African way—the piercing allowed the coin to become a pendant. These pendants were used for protection from evil spirits, as well as in certain religious practices.[11] The resourcefulness of enslaved Africans speaks to their perseverance and illustrates their drive to keep their culture intact in a new and changing world.[12] These artifacts represent the intersections of cook and mistress, black and white, past and present. Such artifacts, along with the still-standing plantation kitchens, the recipes passed down through generations, and now this book, are memorials to those cooks who were bound to the fire for their entire lives.

ACKNOWLEDGMENTS

This book took close to nine years to complete. The journey was supported by countless people and institutions that provided both financial assistance and personal encouragement. I would like to give special thanks to the Rockefeller Library, the Colonial Williamsburg Foundation, the Virginia Historical Society, Randolph College, Roanoke College, the Legacy Museum, and the staffs at the Office for Diversity and Equity at the University of Virginia, Mount Vernon, Monticello, and Poplar Forest for their help over the years. I received professional feedback from Leni Sorensen, Mary V. Thompson, Allison Bell, Lori Lee, Dell Upton, Petrina Jackson, Regina Bush, Jack Gary, Matthew Reeves, Christine Heacock, Doug Samford, Kimberly Phillips, Hermine Pinson, Scott Nelson, Nick Luccketti, and Garrett Fesler. My friends and family were incredibly helpful as well, specifically Barbara Deetz; Trish Deetz; my sisters Tonia Rock, Cricket Deetz, and Cindy Deetz; my brother Eric Deetz and sister-in-law Anna Agbe Davies; Jamiko Hercules; Marilyn Gonzalez; Lalo Gonzalez; Nicole Deetz; Chris Deetz; Wyatt Phipps; Nashiva McDavid; Dan Healy; Katrin Schenk; Alfred Brophy; Julio Rodriguez; Brad Bullock; and Sabita Manian. Gordon Steffey provided immeasurable support throughout this process, for which I am forever indebted. Last, to my son Giacomo, who patiently endured years of my relentless dedication to this project, I thank you.

NOTES

Introduction

1. *Uncle Tom* is a derogatory term for African Americans who align themselves with white cultural values. Aunt Jemima, a well-known grocery icon, has been associated with being less culturally black and more assimilated into white culture. For more on this notion, see Sara Meer, *Uncle Tom Mania: Slavery, Minstrelsy, and Transatlantic Culture in the 1850s* (Athens: University of Georgia Press, 2005).

2. See Marilyn Kern-Foxworth, *Aunt Jemima, Uncle Ben, and Rastus: Blacks in Advertising, Yesterday, Today and Tomorrow* (Westport, CT: Praeger Press, 1994).

3. Ibid.

4. See Katharine E. Harbury, *Colonial Virginia's Cooking Dynasty* (Columbia: University of South Carolina Press, 2004).

5. Anne L. Bower, ed., *African American Foodways: Explorations of History and Culture* (Urbana-Champaign: University of Illinois Press, 2009).

6. James Deetz, *In Small Things Forgotten: The Archaeology of Early American Life* (New York: Doubleday, 1996), 243.

7. Warren M. Billings, *Jamestown and the Founding of the Nation* (Gettysburg, PA: Colonial and National Historic Parks, n.d.), chap. 3.

8. Emily J. Salmon and Edward D. C. Campbell Jr., eds., *The Hornbook of Virginia History* (Richmond: Library of Virginia, 1994), 13–15.

9. Ibid., 13.

10. There are no birth records to document when the first "African American" was born.

11. William Kelso, *Kingsmill Plantations, 1619–1800* (Orlando, FL: Academic Press, 1984), chap. 2.

12. Ira Berlin, *Many Thousands Gone: The First Two Centuries of Slavery in North America* (Cambridge, MA: Belknap Press of Harvard University Press, 1998), chaps. 1, 5.

13. John Hope Franklin and Alfred A. Moss Jr., *From Slavery to Freedom: A History of African Americans,* 8th ed. (Boston: McGraw-Hill, 2000), 65–68.

14. Salmon and Campbell, *Hornbook of Virginia History,* 18.

15. Franklin and Moss, *From Slavery to Freedom,* 66.

16. United States Census and Slave Schedules, 1790, 1820, 1830, 1840, 1860, Historical Census Browser, University of Virginia, Geospatial and Statistical Data Center, http://fisher.lib.virginia.edu/collections/stats/histcensus/index.html.2004 (accessed May 15, 2007; June 28, 2008; March 23 and October 26, 2010).

17. Allan Kulikoff, "The Origins of Afro-American Society in Tidewater Maryland and Virginia, 1700 to 1790," *William and Mary Quarterly,* 3rd ser., 35, no. 2 (April 1978): 231.

18. Joseph E. Holloway, *Africanisms in American Culture* (Bloomington: Indiana University Press, 2005), 31.

19. Gavin Wright, "Slavery and American Agricultural History," *Agricultural History* 77, no. 4 (Autumn 2003): 540–43. For a more detailed account of Virginia's tobacco trends, see Allan Kulikoff, *Tobacco and Slaves: The Development of Southern Cultures in the Chesapeake, 1680–1800* (Williamsburg, VA: Omohundro Institute of Early American History and Culture, 1986).

20. Kulikoff, *Tobacco and Slaves,* introduction.

21. Ibid.

22. See John W. Blassingame, *The Slave Community: Plantation Life in the Antebellum South* (New York: Oxford University Press, 1972); Philip D. Morgan, *Slave Counterpoint: Black Culture in the Eighteenth-Century Chesapeake and Lowcountry* (Williamsburg, VA: Omohundro Institute of Early American History and Culture, 1998); Lawrence W. Levine, *Black Culture and Black Consciousness: Afro-American Folk Thought from Slavery to Freedom* (New York: Oxford University Press, 1977).

1. In Home

1. Dell Upton, "Black and White Landscapes in Eighteenth Century Virginia," in *Material Life in America, 1600–1860,* ed. Robert Blair St. George (Boston: Northeastern University Press, 1988), 357.

2. Cary Carson, "The 'Virginia House' in Maryland," *Maryland Historical Magazine* 69, no. 2 (Summer 1974): 186; Dell Upton, "Early Vernacular Architecture in Southeastern Virginia" (PhD diss., Brown University, 1979), 221, 232.

3. Dell Upton, "Vernacular Domestic Architecture in Eighteenth-Century Virginia," *Winterthur Portfolio* 17, no. 2–3 (Summer–Autumn 1982): 96.

4. Ibid.

5. Michal Sobel, *The World They Made Together: Black and White Values in Eighteenth-Century Virginia* (Princeton, NJ: Princeton University Press, 1987), 44.

6. Upton, "Vernacular Domestic Architecture," 96.

7. Upton, "Black and White Landscapes," 357.

8. Durand de Dauphine, *A Huguenot Exile in Virginia; or, Voyages of a Frenchman Exiled for His Religion, with a Description of Virginia and Maryland,* trans. and ed. Gilbert Chinard (New York: Press of the Pioneers, 1934), 119–20.

9. Cary Carson, "Doing History with Material Culture," in *Material Culture and the Study of American Life,* ed. Ian M. G. Quimby (New York: W. W. Norton, 1978), 52–54, cited in Upton, "Vernacular Domestic Architecture," 102.

10. Robert Beverly, *The History and Present State of Virginia,* ed. Louis B. Wright (Chapel Hill: University of North Carolina Press, 1947), 289–90.

11. John Michael Vlach, *Back of the Big House: The Architecture of Plantation Slavery* (Chapel Hill: University of North Carolina Press, 1993), 43.

12. Ibid.

13. Upton, "Vernacular Domestic Architecture," 96.

14. Ibid., 98.

15. Ibid., 96.

16. Dixon Wecter, *The Saga of American Society: A Record of Social Aspiration 1607–1937* (New York: Charles Scribner's Sons, 1937), 25.

17. Allan Kulikoff, "The Colonial Chesapeake: Seedbed of Antebellum Culture," *Journal of Southern History* 45, no. 4 (November 1979): 534.

18. Cyril M. Harris, ed., *Dictionary of Architecture and Construction,* 3rd ed. (New York: McGraw-Hill, 2000), 424–25.

19. For more on the Georgian mind-set, see Deetz, *In Small Things Forgotten.*

20. Upton, "Vernacular Domestic Architecture," 95.

21. Upton, "Black and White Landscapes," 357.

22. Upton, "Vernacular Domestic Architecture," 95.

23. Ibid., 98.

24. Ibid.

25. Ibid., 102.

26. Ibid.

27. Vlach, *Back of the Big House*, 8.

28. Ibid., chap. 1.

29. Upton, "Vernacular Domestic Architecture," 102.

30. Ibid.

31. Jessica Kross, "Mansions, Men, Women, and the Creation of Multiple Publics in Eighteenth-Century British North America," *Journal of Social History* 33 (Winter 1999): 385.

32. Upton, "Vernacular Domestic Architecture," 103.

33. Ibid., 98.

34. Ibid. 98.

35. Carson, "Doing History with Material Culture," 52–54, cited in Upton, "Vernacular Domestic Architecture," 102.

36. Upton, "Vernacular Domestic Architecture," 104.

37. Ibid., 107, fig. 11.

38. *Virginia Gazette*, 1736–1780, Rockefeller Library, Colonial Williamsburg Foundation, Williamsburg, VA.

39. *Virginia Gazette*, March 21, 1771, 3.

40. Charles Carter Lee Reminiscences, box 9, Charles Carter Lee Papers, University of Virginia, Charlottesville.

41. Upton, "Black and White Landscapes," 359.

42. Ibid., 361.

43. Ibid.

44. Ibid.

45. Ibid.; Whitney L. Battle-Baptiste, "In This Here Place: Interpreting Enslaved Homeplaces," in *Archaeology of Atlantic Africa and the African Diaspora*, ed. Akinwumi Ogundran and Toyin Falola (Bloomington: Indiana University Press, 2007), chap. 10; Sobel, *World They Made Together*, 100.

46. Camille Wells, "The Planter's Prospect: Houses, Outbuildings, and Rural Landscapes in Eighteenth-Century Virginia," *Winterthur Portfolio* 28, no. 1 (Spring 1993): 1–31.

47. Examples can be seen at Thomas Jefferson's Monticello and Bacon's Castle in Surry County, Virginia.

48. Sobel, *World They Made Together*, 127.

49. Mark R. Wenger, "The Dining Room in Early Virginia," *Perspectives in Vernacular Architecture* 3 (1989): 149–59.

50. Upton, "Vernacular Domestic Architecture," 108.

51. Ibid.

52. Upton, "Black and White Landscapes," 361.

53. For descriptions of two of the four major typologies, see Vlach, *Back of the Big House*, 44.

54. See Phillip Vickers Fithian, *Diary, 1747–1776* (Williamsburg, VA: Colonial Williamsburg, 1957), and the citations in chapter 3 for further evidence.

55. See Catherine R. Harrison, Department of Historic Resources file 001-0062, "Willowdale," sec. 7, p. 3, 2007.

56. Upton, "Vernacular Domestic Architecture," 104.

57. Clifton Ellis, "The Mansion House at Berry Hill Plantation: Architecture and the Changing Nature of Slavery in Antebellum Virginia," *Perspectives in Vernacular Architecture* 13, no. 1 (2006): 26.

58. Ibid., 32.

59. Ibid.

60. I use the term *servitude* along with *labor* to stress the performance aspect of enslaved cooks and domestic slaves.

61. Upton, "Vernacular Domestic Architecture," 103.

62. For more on this subject, see Elizabeth Fox-Genovese, *Within the Plantation Household: Black and White Women of the Old South* (Chapel Hill: University of North Carolina Press, 1998).

63. Helen Claire Duprey Bullock, *Kitchens in Colonial Virginia* (Colonial Williamsburg Research Series, 1931), 15.

64. Desiree B. Caldwell, *The Palace Kitchen Report* (Colonial Williamsburg Research Series, 1979).

65. Esther Copley, *Cooks Complete Guide* (London: George Virtue, 1836), 4.

66. Donna C. Hole, *Architectural Fittings in Colonial Virginia* (Colonial Williamsburg Research Series, 1980).

67. Bullock, *Kitchens in Colonial Virginia*, 16.

68. Fithian, *Diary*.

69. See *The African Burial Ground: An American Discovery,* directed by David Kutz (Tribecca Films, 1994).

2. In Labor

1. Mary Randolph, *The Virginia Housewife or, Methodical Cook: A Facsimile of an Authentic Early American Cookbook 1824* (New York: Dover, 1993), 93.

2. Fithian, *Diary,* 99–100.

3. Marion Cabell Tyree, ed., *Housekeeping in Old Virginia* (Louisville, KY: John P. Morton, 1879), 24.

4. Caldwell, *Palace Kitchen Report.*

5. Richard J. Hooker, ed., *Harriot Pinckney Horry Receipt Book, 1770* (Columbia: University of South Carolina Press, 1984), 9.

6. Tyree, *Housekeeping in Old Virginia,* 24.

7. Caldwell, *Palace Kitchen Report.*

8. For more on clothing, see Steve O. Buckridge, *Language of Dress: Resistance and Accommodation in Jamaica 1760–1890* (Kingston, Jamaica: University of West Indies Press, 2004).

9. Richard Eppes Diary, 1858, 20, Virginia Historical Society Manuscript Collections, Richmond.

10. Ibid., 1857–1864.

11. Tyree, *Housekeeping in Old Virginia,* 29.

12. Ibid., 20.

13. Ibid., 98.

14. Ibid.

15. *Virginia Gazette,* December 25, 1779, 2.

16. Randolph, *Virginia Housewife,* 92.

17. Tyree, *Housekeeping in Old Virginia,* 69.

18. Ibid., 211.

19. Randolph, *Virginia Housewife,* 160.

20. Amelia Simmons, *The First American Cookbook: American Cookery* (Albany, NY: C. R. Webster, 1796).

21. Tyree, *Housekeeping in Old Virginia,* 461.

22. Ibid.

23. Deans Family Papers, sec. 1, Virginia Historical Society Manuscript Collections, Richmond.

24. Ibid.

25. Fox-Genovese, *Within the Plantation Household,* 27.

26. Holladay Papers, sec. 234, Virginia Historical Society Manuscript Collections, Richmond.

27. Deans Family Papers, sec. 1.

28. Fox-Genovese, *Within the Plantation Household,* 137.

29. Ibid., 98, 137.

30. For more information, see ibid., 142, where Fox-Genovese quotes Mrs. Merrick's memories of her dealings with the family cook. Since these events occurred outside of Virginia, I omitted them from the text.

31. Jane Francis Walker, *Commonplace Book, Castle Hill Plantation, Albemarle County, Virginia, 1802–1845,* Virginia Historical Society Manuscript Collections, Richmond.

32. It is common knowledge that sugar is addictive and that its consumption causes psychophysical reactions in most people. See http://www.princeton.edu/pr/news/02/q2/0620-hoebel.htm.

33. Eppes Diary, 1857, 322.

34. *Virginia Gazette,* March 24, 1775, 4.

35. *Virginia Gazette,* April 25, 1751, 4.

36. Charles Purdue, *Weevils in the Wheat: Interviews with Virginia's Ex-Slaves* (Charlottesville: University of Virginia Press, 1977), 275.

37. Ibid., 154.

38. Ibid., 63.

39. Jacqueline Jones, *Labor of Love, Labor of Sorrow: Black Women, Work, and the Family from Slavery to the Present* (New York: Basic Books, 1995), 61.

40. *Virginia Gazette,* November 24, 1768, 3.

41. *Virginia Gazette,* July 27, 1769, 3.

42. *Virginia Gazette,* September 26, 1771, 4.

43. *Virginia Gazette,* November 25, 1773, 4.

44. Spragins Family Papers, 1753–1781, sec. 67, Virginia Historical Society Manuscript Collections, Richmond.

45. David Hunter Strother, *Harper's New Monthly Magazine,* January 1856, 176–77.

46. Deans Family Papers, sec. 1 (referring to back-stage service staff).

47. Ibid.

48. Ibid.

49. Ibid.

50. Ibid.

51. Fithian, *Diary*, 93.

52. Ibid., 82.

53. Eleanor Beverly Platt, letter, December 31, 1864, Virginia Historical Society Manuscript Collections, Richmond.

54. Purdue, *Weevils in the Wheat*, 158.

55. Ibid., 83.

56. Eppes Diary, 1856.

57. Eppes Diary, 1858, 45.

58. Frederick Olmsted, *A Journey in the Seaboard Slave States: With Remarks on Their Economy* (London: Samson Low, Sons, & Co., 1856), 395.

3. In Fame and Fear

1. "Hansons [*sic*] Mode of Making Chicken Broth; the Best in the World," in *Nelly Custis Lewis's Housekeeping Book*, 73, in Mary V. Thompson, comp., *Slaves at Mount Vernon in 1799: Slaves on the Mansion House Farm–1799* (Mount Vernon Ladies' Association, 1992–April 4, 1997; additional material added July 24, 2003–May 26, 2015).

2. "Hanson's Thin Biscuits," ibid., 85.

3. "Hansons [*sic*] Breakfast Biscuits," ibid.

4. Martha Washington to Mrs. Elizabeth Powel, May 20, 1797, in *The Worthy Partner: The Papers of Martha Washington,* ed. Joseph E. Fields (Westport, CT: Greenwood Press, 1994), 302, 303n.

5. George Washington, "Memorandum: List of Tithables, 14 June 1771," Founders Online, National Archives, http://founders.archives .gov/documents/Washington/02-08-02 -0325 (last modified March 30, 2017)—original source: *The Papers of George Washington, Colonial Series,* vol. 8, *24 June 1767–25 December 1771,* ed. W. W. Abbot and Dorothy Twohig (Charlottesville: University Press of Virginia, 1993), 479–80; *Information on Mount Vernon Slaves Who Died, Were Sold, or Escaped Prior to the Summer of 1799 and the Compilation of George Washington's Final Slave List* (Mount Vernon Ladies' Association, September 2, 2005–January 6, 2015), courtesy of Mary V. Thompson.

6. George Washington, diary entry, February 18, 1786, Founders Online, http://founders.archives.gov/documents/Washington/01-04-02-0003-0002-0018. Original source: *The Diaries of George Washington*, vol. 4, *1 September 1784–30 June 1786*, ed. Donald Jackson and Dorothy Twohig (Charlottesville: University Press of Virginia, 1978), 276–83.

7. See entry dated September 9, 1787, in Mount Vernon Storehouse Account Book (bound manuscript), Mount Vernon Ladies' Association, courtesy of Mary V. Thompson; *Information on Mount Vernon Slaves*.

8. George Washington, "Memorandum: List of Tithables, July 1774," Founders Online, http://founders.archives.gov/documents/Washington/02-10-02- 0085—original source: *Papers of George Washington, Colonial Series*, vol. 10, *21 March 1774–15 June 1775*, ed. W. W. Abbot and Dorothy Twohig (Charlottesville: University Press of Virginia, 1995), 137–38; *Information on Mount Vernon Slaves*.

9. "From George Washington to Tobias Lear, 9 September 1790," Founders Online, http://founders.archives.gov/documents/Washington/05-06-02-0195. Original source: *The Papers of George Washington, Presidential Series*, vol. 6, *1 July 1790–30 November 1790*, ed. Mark A. Mastromarino (Charlottesville: University Press of Virginia, 1996), 408–10.

10. "From George Washington to Tobias Lear, 17 September 1790," Founders Online, http://founders.archives.gov/documents/Washington/05-06-02-0216. Original source: *Papers of George Washington, Presidential Series*, 6:465–67.

11. "To George Washington from Tobias Lear, 14 November 1790," Founders Online, http:/founders.archives.gov/documents/Washington/05-06-02-0315. Original source: *Papers of George Washington, Presidential Series*, 6:655–58.

12. "From George Washington to Tobias Lear, 22 November 1790," Founders Online, http://founders.archives.gov/documents/Washington/05-06-02-0331. Original source: *Papers of George Washington, Presidential Series*, 6:682–83.

13. Stephen Decatur, *Private Affairs of George Washington from the Records and Accounts of Tobias Lear, Esquire, His Secretary* (Boston: Houghton Mifflin, 1933), 169.

14. "From George Washington to Tobias Lear, 27 March 1791," Founders Online, http://founders.archives.gov/documents/Washington/05-08-02-0011. Original source: *The Papers of George Washington, Presidential Series*, vol. 8, *22 March 1791–22 September 1791*, ed. Mark A. Mastromarino (Charlottesville: University Press of Virginia, 1999), 17–19.

15. "To George Washington from Tobias Lear, 17 April 1791," Founders Online, http://founders.archives.gov/documents/Washington/05-08-02-0090. Original source: *Papers of George Washington, Presidential Series*, 8:120–22.

16. Ibid.

17. "To George Washington from Tobias Lear, 24 April 1791," Founders Online, http://founders.archives.gov/documents/Washington/05-08-02-0099. Original source: *Papers of George Washington, Presidential Series*, 8:129–34.

18. "From George Washington to Tobias Lear, 12 April 1791," Founders Online, http://founders.archives.gov/documents/Washington/05-08-02-0062. Original source: *Papers of George Washington, Presidential Series*, 8:84–86.

19. Tobias Lear to George Washington, Philadelphia, April 24, 1791, in *Papers of George Washington, Presidential Series*, 8:131–32.

20. Ibid.

21. "Tobias Lear to Daniel Grant, 28 February 1790," Founders Online, http://founders.archives.gov/documents/Washington/05-05-02-0113. Original source: *The Papers of George Washington, Presidential Series*, vol. 5, *16 January 1790–30 June 1790*, ed. Dorothy Twohig, Mark A. Mastromarino, and Jack D. Warren (Charlottesville: University Press of Virginia, 1996), 185–87.

22. Tobias Lear to George Washington, Philadelphia, June 5, 1791, in *Papers of George Washington, Presidential Series*, 8:232, 233n–234n.

23. Tobias Lear to George Washington, Philadelphia, May 15, 1791, ibid., 8:189–90.

24. George Washington Parke Custis, *Recollections and Private Memoirs of Washington* (New York: Derby & Jackson, 1860), 422–24.

25. George Washington to his farm manager, William Pearce, Philadelphia, November 14, 1796, in *The Writings of George Washington, 14 vols. ed. Worthington Chauncey Ford* (New York: G. P. Putnam's Sons, 1889–1893), http://oll.libertyfund.org/titles/2348.

26. Weekly Report, February 25, 1797, in Mount Vernon Weekly Reports, January 7, 1797–September 10, 1797, Fred W. Smith National Library for the Study of George Washington, Mount Vernon.

27. "To George Washington from Frederick Kitt, 15 January 1798," Founders Online, http://founders.archives.gov/documents/Washington/06-02-02-0026. Original source: *The Papers of George Washington, Retirement Series*, vol. 2, *2 January 1798–15 September 1798*, ed. W. W. Abbot (Charlottesville: University Press of Virginia, 1998), 25–26.

28. "From George Washington to Frederick Kitt, 10 January 1798," Founders Online, http:/founders.archives.gov/documents/Washington/06-02-02-0016. Original source: *Papers of George Washington, Retirement Series*, 2:16.

29. Martha Washington to Colonel Richard Varick, Mount Vernon, December 15, 1801, in Fields, *Worthy Partner*, 398, 399n.

30. Mr. Lewis's "List of the Different Drafts of Negros," [1802], manuscript letterbook, 1800–1829, Peter Family Collection, Fred W. Smith National Library for the Study of George Washington.

31. Mrs. Law's "List of the Different Drafts of Negros," [1802], Peter Family Collection, Fred W. Smith National Library for the Study of George Washington; *Slaves on the River Farm—1799*, courtesy of Mary V. Thompson.

32. Louis-Philippe (king of France, 1830–1848), *Diary of My Travels in America*, trans. Stephen Becker (New York: Delacorte Press, 1977), 32. This "six-year-old" was likely Evey, who would have been thirteen in 1797 but was listed as a dwarf in Washington's papers.

33. See Annette Gordon-Reed, *The Hemingses of Monticello: An American Family* (New York: W. W. Norton, 2008); Thomas J. Craughtwell, *Thomas Jefferson's Crème Brulee: How a Founding Father and His Slave James Hemings Introduced French Cuisine to America* (Philadelphia: Quirk Books, 2012).

34. William Evans to Thomas Jefferson, November 5, 1801, in *The Papers of Thomas Jefferson*, ed. Julian P. Boyd, Charles T. Cullen, John Catanzariti, Barbara B. Oberg, et al. (Princeton, NJ: Princeton University Press, 1950), 35:569–70.

35. *Virginia Gazette*, March 26, 1779, 3.

36. Katherine G. Revell, *Research Report with Recommendations*

for Reinterpreting and Refurnishing Monticello's Kitchen and Related Dependencies (Jefferson Library, Thomas Jefferson Memorial Foundation, 1996).

37. See Gordon-Reed, *Hemingses of Monticello;* Craughtwell, *Thomas Jefferson's Crème Brulee.*

38. Revell, *Research Report,* vol. 2.

39. Philip J. Schwartz, *Twice Condemned: Slaves and the Criminal Laws of Virginia, 1705–1865* (Baton Rouge: Louisiana State University Press, 1988), 97.

40. Ibid., 101. For a detailed account of the cases, see ibid., chap. 4.

41. For more on dyes and remedies, see Walker, *Commonplace Book;* Charles Dabney, *Commonplace Book, 1811–1825,* Dabney Family Papers, Virginia Historical Society Manuscript Collections, Richmond.

42. Walker, *Commonplace Book.* See also Dabney, *Commonplace Book.*

43. Holly Phaneuf, *Herbs Demystified* (New York: Marlow, 2005).

44. See Lorena S. Walsh, *From Calabar to Carter's Grove: The History of a Virginia Slave Community* (Charlottesville: University of Virginia Press, 1997); Douglas B. Chambers, *Murder at Montpelier: Igbo African in Virginia* (Jackson: University of Mississippi Press, 2005).

45. Chambers, *Murder at Montpelier,* 14.

46. "The Burning of Eve," *Virginia Magazine of History and Biography* 3 (January 1896): 103.

47. Glenn McNair, *Criminal Injustice: Slaves and Free Blacks in Georgia's Criminal Justice System* (Charlottesville: University of Virginia Press, 2009), 63; Schwartz, *Twice Condemned,* 95.

48. See http://deathpenaltyusa.org/usa1/indexstate1.htm (accessed May 20, 2015).

49. Essex County Court Orders, no. 48, 1833–1836, reel 97, Library of Virginia, Richmond.

50. Ibid.

51. Ibid.

52. Auditor of Public Accounts, Condemned Blacks Executed and Transported, October 28, 1834, miscellaneous reel 2549, and Condemned Slaves, Court Orders, and Valuations, 1833–1835, miscellaneous reel 2553, pp. 0160–0161, Library of Virginia, Richmond.

53. Chancery Court Papers, petition 21683420, box 38, folder 37-1834, Library of Virginia, Richmond.

54. Fithian, *Diary,* 252.

55. Robert L. Crewdson, James P. Whittenburg, and John M. Coski, *Charles City County Virginia, an Official History: Four Centuries of the Southern Experience; Charles City County, Virginia, from the Age of Discovery to the Modern Civil Rights Struggle* (Salem, WV: Don Mills, 1989), 65.

56. John R. Hicks, "African Consumption," *Stethoscope* 4 (November 1854); Hicks, "Medico-Chirurgical Society of the City of Richmond—First March Meeting," *Stethoscope and Virginia Medicine Gazette* 3 (April 1853).

4. In Dining

1. Mary H. Randolph to her sister, November 26, 1827, Randolph de Potestad Family Papers, folder 1, p. 2, Rockefeller Library, Colonial Williamsburg Foundation.

2. Tyree, *Housekeeping in Old Virginia,* vii.

3. Wecter, *Saga of American Society,* 22.

4. Ibid., 23.

5. Joe Gray Taylor, *Eating, Drinking, and Visiting in the South: An Informal History* (Baton Rouge: Louisiana State University Press, 1982), 60.

6. See Kross, "Mansions, Men, Women."

7. Ibid., 385.

8. See Rhys Isaac, *The Transformation of Virginia 1740–1790* (Williamsburg, VA: Omohundro Institute of Early American History and Culture, 1984).

9. Kross, "Mansions, Men, Women," 385.

10. Sobel, *World They Made Together,* 151.

11. Kross, "Mansions, Men, Women," 386–87.

12. See Ellis, "Mansion House at Berry Hill Plantation."

13. See Fithian, *Diary.*

14. See Thavolia Glymph, *Out of the House of Bondage: The Transformation of the Plantation Household* (Cambridge: Cambridge University Press, 2008).

15. Randolph de Potestad Family Papers, 1826–1913, folder 1, Rockefeller Library, Colonial Williamsburg Foundation.

16. Tyree, *Housekeeping in Old Virginia,* front cover.

17. Ibid., proverb xxxi, 10, 27.

18. Glymph, *Out of the House of Bondage*, chap. 2.

19. Fox-Genovese, *Within the Plantation Household*, 61.

20. Jane Watkins Edmunds, Berkeley, letter to nanny, Edmunds Family Papers, sec. 3, Virginia Historical Society Manuscript Collections, Richmond.

21. Beverly, *History and Present State of Virginia*, 292.

22. Tyree, *Housekeeping in Old Virginia*, viii.

23. Ibid., xli.

24. Mrs. T. J. B. T. Worthington's recollections, 1861–1865, Bryan Family Papers, sec. 5, pp. 1–5, Virginia Historical Society Manuscript Collections, Richmond.

25. Henry C. Knight, "A New England Poet in Virginia and Kentucky, 1819," in *A Mirror for Americans,* ed. Warren S. Tyron (Chicago: University of Chicago Press, 1952), 259.

26. Ibid., 260.

27. Ibid., 261.

28. Pine Grove Diary, January 4, 1854, Virginia Historical Society Manuscript Collections, Richmond.

29. Ibid., January 7 and 8, 1854.

30. Tyree, *Housekeeping in Old Virginia*, 19.

31. Anne Frior Scott, *The Southern Lady, from Pedestal to Politics, 1830–1930* (Chicago: University of Chicago Press, 1970), 8.

32. Elizabeth Langhorn, K. Edward Lay, and William D. Reilly, eds., *A Virginia Family and Its Plantation Houses* (Charlottesville: University of Virginia Press, 1987), 30–31.

33. Linda E. Parris, *A Dutiful Obedient Wife: The Journal of Elizabeth Foote Washington* (Williamsburg, VA: College of William and Mary, 1984), 32.

34. Quoted in ibid., 66.

35. Scott, *Southern Lady*, 6.

36. Ibid., 10, 19, 29.

37. Ibid., x.

38. Fox-Genovese, *Within the Plantation Household*, 84.

39. Scott, *Southern Lady*, 31.

40. Maria Octavia Selden Nelson, Schoolbook, 1845, Virginia Historical Society Manuscript Collections, Richmond.

41. These terms varied, depending on the plantation. *Breakfast* was always the morning meal; *supper* and *dinner* were used interchangeably for the afternoon or evening meal; and *tea,* consisting of a snack and a hot drink, usually occurred in the afternoon, sometimes taking the place of the middle meal. For the sake of clarity, *supper* is used here for the evening meal, and *dinner* for the afternoon meal.

42. Fithian, *Diary,* 41.

43. Ibid.

44. Quoted in Carole McCabe, "Woodlawn Hospitality," *Early American Life* 19, no. 1 (February 1988): 58.

45. Fithian, *Diary,* 45.

46. Quoted in Langhorn et al., *A Virginia Family and Its Plantation Houses,* 102.

47. Quoted in McCabe, "Woodlawn Hospitality," 58–70.

48. Susan Pinkard, *A Revolution in Taste: The Rise of French Cuisine* (Cambridge: Cambridge University Press, 2009), 125.

49. Hooker, *Harriot Pinckney Horry Receipt Book,* 19.

50. Knight, "New England Poet in Virginia and Kentucky," 261.

51. Olmsted, *Journey in the Seaboard Slave States,* 353.

52. Wecter, *Saga of American Society,* 25–26.

53. *Virginia Gazette,* October 7, 1737, 4.

54. *Virginia Gazette,* October 21, 1737, 4.

55. McCabe, "Woodlawn Hospitality," 58.

56. John Young Mason, Account Book, 1839, Virginia Historical Society Manuscript Collections, Richmond.

57. McCabe, "Woodlawn Hospitality," 58.

58. George Blow to John Y. Mason, January 1832, Mason Family Papers, sec. 6, folder 3/37, Virginia Historical Society Manuscript Collections, Richmond.

59. Tyree, *Housekeeping in Old Virginia,* ix–x.

60. Eppes Diary, 1858.

61. *Virginia Gazette,* March 8, 1770, 3.

62. *Virginia Gazette,* April 11, 1777, 2.

63. Fox-Genovese, *Within the Plantation Household,* 64.

64. Deans Family Papers, sec. 1.

65. Randolph, *Virginia Housewife,* 96.

66. See Kelley Deetz, "Stolen Bodies, Edible Memories: The In-

fluences and Function of West African Foodways in the Early British Atlantic," in *Routledge History of Food*, ed. Carol Helstosky (London: Routledge, 2014); James C. McCain, *Stirring the Pot: A History of African Cuisine* (Athens: Ohio University Press, 2009).

67. McCain, *Stirring the Pot.*

68. Chambers, *Murder at Montpelier*, 40.

69. Ibid., 166.

70. Maria Franklin, "The Archaeological Dimensions of Soul Food: Interpreting Race, Culture, and Afro-Virginian Identity," in *Race and the Archaeology of Identity*, ed. Charles Orser Jr. (Salt Lake City: University of Utah Press, 2001).

5. In Memory

1. Booker T. Washington, *Up from Slavery* (Boston: Bedford/St. Martin's, 2003), 281.

2. *Virginia Gazette*, November 27, 1778, 3.

3. *Virginia Gazette*, October 20, 1774, supplement, 2.

4. *Virginia Gazette*, April 14, 1775, 3.

5. *Virginia Gazette*, February 12, 1780, 3.

6. *Virginia Gazette*, February 16, 1776, 3.

7. Jones, *Labor of Love, Labor of Sorrow*, 14, 11, 30, 28.

8. Gibson Jefferson McConnaughey, *Two Centuries of Virginia Cooking* (Amelia, VA: Mid-South Publishing, 1978), 8.

9. James Deetz, *Flowerdew Hundred: The Archaeology of a Virginia Plantation 1619–1864* (Charlottesville: University Press of Virginia, 1993), 135–37.

10. Mark P. Leone and Gladys Marie Fry, "Conjuring in the Big House Kitchen," *Journal of American Folklore* 112, no. 445 (1999): 372–403.

11. Ibid. Also see Albert J. Raboteau, *Slave Religion: The Invisible Institution in the American South* (Oxford: Oxford University Press, 1980).

12. Although these few artifacts do not prove Africans' resourcefulness or perseverance, they do provide tangible evidence that supports the scholarly work presented in Raboteau, *Slave Religion;* Blassingame, *Slave Community;* Berlin, *Many Thousands Gone;* Chambers, *Murder at*

Montpelier; and Sobel, *World They Made Together,* as well as the film *The African Burial Ground: An American Discovery,* directed by David Kutz (Tribecca Films, 1994).

BIBLIOGRAPHY

Papers and Collections

Auditor of Public Accounts, Condemned Blacks Executed and Transported, October 28, 1834, and Condemned Slaves, Court Orders, and Valuations, 1833–1835. Library of Virginia, Richmond.

Bryan Family Papers. Virginia Historical Society Manuscript Collections, Richmond.

Chancery Court Papers. Library of Virginia, Richmond.

Dabney Family Papers. Virginia Historical Society Manuscript Collections, Richmond.

Deans Family Papers. Virginia Historical Society Manuscript Collections, Richmond.

Dixon Archaeological Collection. James River Institute for Archaeology, Williamsburg, VA.

Edmunds Family Papers. Virginia Historical Society Manuscript Collections, Richmond.

Eppes, Richard, Diaries, 1857–1864. Virginia Historical Society Manuscript Collections, Richmond.

Essex County Court Orders. Library of Virginia, Richmond.

Flowerdew Hundred Collection Papers. University of Virginia Special Collections at Morven.

Holladay Papers. Virginia Historical Society Manuscript Collections, Richmond.

Lee, Charles Carter, Papers. University of Virginia, Charlottesville.

Mason, John Young, Account Book, 1839. Virginia Historical Society Manuscript Collections, Richmond.

Mason Family Papers. Virginia Historical Society Manuscript Collections, Richmond.

National Park Service National Register of Historic Places Registration Form. Department of Historic Preservation, United States Department of the Interior, Richmond, VA.

Nelson, Maria Octavia Selden, Schoolbook, 1845. Virginia Historical Society Manuscript Collections, Richmond.

Peter Family Collection. Special Collections, Fred W. Smith National Library for the Study of George Washington, Mount Vernon.

Pine Grove Diary. Virginia Historical Society Manuscript Collections, Richmond.

Platt, Eleanor Beverly, Letter, December 31, 1864. Virginia Historical Society Manuscript Collections, Richmond.

Randolph de Potestad Family Papers, 1826–1913. Rockefeller Library, Colonial Williamsburg Foundation.

Spragins Family Papers, 1753–1881. Virginia Historical Society Manuscript Collections, Richmond.

United States Census and Slave Schedules, 1790, 1820, 1830, 1840, 1860. Historical Census Browser, University of Virginia, Geospatial and Statistical Data Center. http://fisher.lib.virginia.edu/collections/stats/histcensus/index.html.

Walker, Jane Francis. *Commonplace Book, Castle Hill Plantation, Albemarle County, Virginia, 1802–1845.* Virginia Historical Society Manuscript Collections, Richmond.

Washington, George, Papers. University of Virginia. http://gwpapers.virginia.edu/.

Archaeological Sites

Buckhorn Manor, State Route 603, Bacova vicinity, Bath County, VA.

Chatham Kitchen, Stafford County, VA.

Green Hill Plantation, State Route 728, Long Island vicinity, Campbell County, VA.

Kendall Grove, State Route 674, Eastville vicinity, Northampton County, VA.

Kenmore Kitchen, 1201 Washington Avenue, Fredericksburg, VA.

Westover Kitchen Building, State Route 633, Charles City vicinity, Charles City County, VA.

Bibliography

Books, Articles, and Dissertations

Aptheker, Herbert. *American Negro Slave Revolts*. New York: Columbia University Press, 1943.

Battle-Baptiste, Whitney L. "In This Here Place: Interpreting Enslaved Homeplaces." In *Archaeology of Atlantic Africa and the African Diaspora*, ed. Akinwumi Ogundrian and Toyin Falola. Bloomington: Indiana University Press, 2007.

Berlin, Ira. *Many Thousands Gone: The First Two Centuries of Slavery in North America*. Cambridge, MA: Belknap Press of Harvard University Press, 1998.

———. *Slaves without Masters: The Free Negro in the Antebellum South*. New York: Pantheon Books, 1975.

Berlin, Ira, Marc Favreau, and Stephen F. Miller, eds. *Remembering Slavery*. New York: New Press, 1998.

Beverly, Robert. *The History and Present State of Virginia*. Edited by Louis B. Wright. Chapel Hill: University of North Carolina Press, 1947.

Billings, Warren M. *Jamestown and the Founding of the Nation*. Gettysburg, PA: Colonial and National Historic Parks, n.d.

Blassingame, John W. *The Slave Community: Plantation Life in the Antebellum South*. New York: Oxford University Press, 1972.

———. *Slave Testimony: Two Centuries of Letters, Speeches, Interviews and Autobiographies*. Baton Rouge: Louisiana State University Press, 1977.

Bower, Anne L., ed. *African American Foodways: Explorations of History and Culture*. Urbana-Champaign: University of Illinois Press, 2009.

Brown, Kathleen M. *Good Wives, Nasty Wenches, and Anxious Patriarchs*. Chapel Hill: University of North Carolina Press, 1996.

Buckridge, Steve O. *Language of Dress: Resistance and Accommodation in Jamaica 1760–1890*. Kingston, Jamaica: University of West Indies Press, 2004.

Bullock, Helen Claire Duprey. *Kitchens in Colonial Virginia*. Colonial Williamsburg Research Series, 1931.

"The Burning of Eve." *Virginia Magazine of History and Biography* 3 (January 1896): 310–11.

Bibliography

Caldwell, Desiree B. *The Palace Kitchen Report*. Colonial Williamsburg Research Series, 1979.

Carson, Cary. "Doing History with Material Culture." In *Material Culture and the Study of American Life*, ed. Ian M. G. Quimby. New York: W. W. Norton, 1978.

———. "The 'Virginia House' in Maryland." *Maryland Historical Magazine* 69, no. 2 (Summer 1974): 185–96.

Chambers, Douglas B. *Murder at Montpelier: Igbo African in Virginia*. Jackson: University of Mississippi Press, 2005.

Collins, Patricia Hill. *Black Feminist Thought*. 2nd ed. New York: Routlege, 2000.

Copley, Esther. *Cooks Complete Guide*. London: George Virtue, 1836.

Craughtwell, Thomas J. *Thomas Jefferson's Crème Brule: How a Founding Father and His Slave James Hemings Introduced French Cuisine to America*. Philadelphia: Quirk Books, 2012.

Crewdson, Robert L., James P. Whittenburg, and John M. Coski. *Charles City County Virginia, an Official History: Four Centuries of the Southern Experience; Charles City County, Virginia, from the Age of Discovery to the Modern Civil Rights Struggle*. Salem, WV: Don Mills, 1989.

Crump, Nancy Carter. *Hearthside Cooking*. McLean, VA: EPM Publishing, 1985.

Curtin, Philip D. *The Atlantic Slave Trade: A Census*. Madison: University of Wisconsin Press, 1969.

Curtin, Philip D., and Paul E. Lovejoy, eds. *Africans in Bondage: Studies in Slavery and the Slave Trade*. Madison: University of Wisconsin Press, 1986.

Curtin, Philip De Armond, ed. *Africa Remembered: Narratives by West Africans from the Era of the Slave Trade*. Prospect Heights, IL: Waveland Press, 1997.

Custis, George Washington Parke. *Recollections and Private Memoirs of Washington*. New York: Derby & Jackson, 1860.

Decatur, Stephen. *Private Affairs of George Washington from the Records and Accounts of Tobias Lear, Esquire, His Secretary*. Boston: Houghton Mifflin, 1933.

de Dauphine, Durand. *A Huguenot Exile in Virginia; or, Voyages of a Frenchman Exiled for His Religion, with a Description of Virginia and*

Maryland. Translated and edited by Gilbert Chinard. New York: Press of the Pioneers, 1934.

Deetz, James. *Flowerdew Hundred: The Archaeology of a Virginia Plantation 1619–1864.* Charlottesville: University Press of Virginia, 1993.

———. *In Small Things Forgotten: The Archaeology of Early American Life.* New York: Doubleday, 1996.

Deetz, Kelley. "Stolen Bodies, Edible Memories: The Influences and Function of West African Foodways in the Early British Atlantic." In *Routledge History of Food,* ed. Carol Helstosky. London: Routledge, 2014.

DuBois, W. E. B. *The Souls of Black Folks.* Boston: Bedford Books, 1997.

Elkins, Stanley M. *Slavery: A Problem in American Institutional and Intellectual Life.* Chicago: University of Chicago Press, 1976.

Ellis, Clifton. "The Mansion House at Berry Hill Plantation: Architecture and the Changing Nature of Slavery in Antebellum Virginia." *Perspectives in Vernacular Architecture* 13, no. 1 (2006): 22–48.

Eltis, David. *The Rise of African Slavery in the Americas.* Cambridge: Cambridge University Press, 2000.

Epperson, Terrence. "Race and the Disciplines of the Plantation." *Historical Archaeology* 24, no. 4 (1990): 29–36.

Equiano, Olaudah. *The Interesting Narrative of the Life of Olaudah Equiano.* Boston: Bedford Books of St. Martin's Press, 1995.

Fairbanks, Charles. "The Kingsley Slave Cabins in Duval County, Florida, 1968, and the Plantation Archaeology of the Southeastern Coast." *Historical Archaeology* 18, no. 1 (1984): 62–93.

Fields, Joseph E., ed. *The Worthy Partner: The Papers of Martha Washington.* Westport, CT: Greenwood Press, 1994.

Fithian, Phillip Vickers. *Diary, 1747–1776.* Williamsburg, VA: Colonial Williamsburg, 1957.

Fogel, Rodger W., and Stanley L. Engerman. *Time on the Cross: The Economics of American Negro Slavery.* Boston: Little Brown, 1974.

Fox-Genovese, Elizabeth. *Within the Plantation Household: Black and White Women of the Old South.* Chapel Hill: University of North Carolina Press, 1998.

Franklin, John Hope, and Alfred A. Moss Jr. *From Slavery to Freedom: A History of African Americans.* 8th ed. Boston: McGraw-Hill, 2000.

Franklin, Maria. "The Archaeological Dimensions of Soul Food: Interpreting Race, Culture, and Afro-Virginian Identity." In *Race and the Archaeology of Identity*, ed. Charles Orser Jr. Salt Lake City: University of Utah Press, 2001.

Frazier, E. Franklin. *The Negro in the United States*. New York: Macmillan, 1949.

Frey, Sylvia R., and Betty Wood. *From Slavery to Emancipation in the Atlantic World*. London: Frank Cass, 1999.

Galle, Jillian, and Amy Young, eds. *Engendering African American Archaeology: A Southern Perspective*. Knoxville: University of Tennessee Press, 2004.

Gaspar, David Barry, and Darlene Clark Hines, eds. *More than Chattel: Black Women and Slavery in the Americas*. Bloomington: Indiana University Press, 1996.

Gates, Henry Louis, ed. *The Classic Slave Narratives*. New York: Penguin, 1987.

Genovese, Eugene. *Roll, Jordan, Roll: The World the Slaves Made*. New York: Pantheon Books, 1974.

Glymph, Thavolia. *Out of the House of Bondage: The Transformation of the Plantation Household*. Cambridge: Cambridge University Press, 2008.

Gomez, Michael A. *Exchanging Our Country Marks: The Transformation of African Identities in the Colonial and Antebellum South*. Chapel Hill: University of North Carolina Press, 1998.

Gordon-Reed, Annette. *The Hemingses of Monticello: An American Family*. New York: W. W. Norton, 2008.

Harbury, Katharine E. *Colonial Virginia's Cooking Dynasty*. Columbia: University of South Carolina Press, 2004.

Harris, Cyril M., ed. *Dictionary of Architecture and Construction*. 3rd ed. New York: McGraw-Hill, 2000.

Harris, Jessica B. *High on the Hog: A Cultural Journey from Africa to America*, New York: Bloomsbury, 2011.

Hess, Karen. *Martha Washington's Booke of Cookery*. New York: Columbia University Press, 1995.

Hicks, John R. "African Consumption." *Stethoscope* 4 (November 1854).

———. "Medico-Chirurgical Society of the City of Richmond—First March Meeting." *Stethoscope and Virginia Medicine Gazette* 3 (April 1853).

Hogendorn, Jan S. *The Shell Money of the Slave Trade.* Cambridge: Cambridge University Press, 1986.

Hole, Donna C. *Architectural Fittings in Colonial Virginia.* Colonial Williamsburg Research Series, 1980.

Holloway, Joseph E. *Africanisms in American Culture.* Bloomington: Indiana University Press, 2005.

Hooker, Richard J., ed. *Harriot Pinckney Horry Receipt Book, 1770.* Columbia: University of South Carolina Press, 1984.

Howson, Jean E. "Social Relations and Material Culture: A Critique of the Archaeology of Plantation Slavery." *Historical Archaeology* 24, no. 4 (1990): 72–91.

Hume, Ivor Noel. *A Guide to Artifacts of Colonial America.* Philadelphia: University of Pennsylvania Press, 1969.

Inikori, Joseph E., and Stanley L. Engerman, eds. *The Atlantic Slave Trade: Effects on Economies, Societies, and Peoples in Africa, the Americas, and Europe.* Durham, NC: Duke University Press, 1992.

Isaac, Rhys. *The Transformation of Virginia 1740–1790.* Williamsburg, VA: Omohundro Institute of Early American History and Culture, 1984.

Jacobs, Harriet A., and Jean F. Yellen, eds. *Incidents in the Life of a Slave Girl: Written by Herself.* Cambridge, MA: Harvard University Press, 1987.

Jefferson, Thomas. *The Papers of Thomas Jefferson.* Edited by Julian P. Boyd, Charles T. Cullen, John Catanzariti, Barbara B. Oberg, et al. Princeton, NJ: Princeton University Press, 1950.

Jones, Jacqueline. *Labor of Love, Labor of Sorrow: Black Women, Work, and the Family from Slavery to the Present.* New York: Basic Books, 1995.

Kelso, William. *Kingsmill Plantations, 1619–1800.* Orlando, FL: Academic Press, 1984.

Kern-Foxworth, Marilyn. *Aunt Jemima, Uncle Ben, and Rastus: Blacks in Advertising, Yesterday, Today, and Tomorrow.* Westport, CT: Praeger Press, 1994.

King, Wilma. *Stolen Childhood: Slave Youth in Nineteenth-Century America.* Bloomington: Indiana University Press, 1995.

Klein, Herbert S. *The Atlantic Slave Trade.* New York: Cambridge University Press, 1999.

Klingberg, Frank J. "Carter Godwin Woodson, Historian, and His Contribution to American Historiography." *Journal of Negro History* 41, no. 1 (January 1956): 66–68.

Knight, Henry C. "A New England Poet in Virginia and Kentucky, 1819." In *A Mirror for Americans,* ed. Warren S. Tyron. Chicago: University of Chicago Press, 1952.

Kross, Jessica. "Mansions, Men, Women, and the Creation of Multiple Publics in Eighteenth-Century British North America." *Journal of Social History* 33 (Winter 1999): 385–408.

Kulikoff, Allan. "The Colonial Chesapeake: Seedbed of Antebellum Culture." *Journal of Southern History* 45, no. 4 (November 1979): 513–40.

———. "The Origins of Afro-American Society in Tidewater Maryland and Virginia, 1700 to 1790." *William and Mary Quarterly,* 3rd ser., 35, no. 2 (April 1978): 226–59.

———. *Tobacco and Slaves: The Development of Southern Cultures in the Chesapeake, 1680–1800.* Williamsburg, VA: Omohundro Institute of Early American History and Culture, 1986.

Langhorn, Elizabeth, K. Edward Lay, and William D. Reilly, eds. *A Virginia Family and Its Plantation Houses.* Charlottesville: University of Virginia Press, 1987.

Leone, Mark P., and Gladys Marie Fry. "Conjuring in the Big House Kitchen." *Journal of American Folklore* 112, no. 445 (1999): 372–403.

Levine, Lawrence W. *Black Culture and Black Consciousness: Afro-American Folk Thought from Slavery to Freedom.* New York: Oxford University Press, 1977.

Louis-Philippe. *Diary of My Travels in America.* Translated by Stephen Becker. New York: Delacorte Press, 1977.

Lovejoy, Paul E., and Nicholas Rogers, eds. *Unfree Labour in the Development of the Atlantic World.* London: Frank Cass, 1994.

Manning, Marable, M. *Slave in a Box: The Strange Career of Aunt Jemima.* Charlottesville: University of Virginia Press, 1998.

McCabe, Carole. "Woodlawn Hospitality." *Early American Life* 19, no. 1 (February 1988): 58–70.

McCain, James C. *Stirring the Pot: A History of African Cuisine.* Athens: Ohio University Press, 2009.

McConnaughey, Gibson Jefferson. *Two Centuries of Virginia Cooking.* Amelia, VA: Mid-South Publishing, 1978.

McNair, Glenn. *Criminal Injustice: Slaves and Free Blacks in Georgia's Criminal Justice System.* Charlottesville: University of Virginia Press, 2009.

Meer, Sara. *Uncle Tom Mania: Slavery, Minstrelsy, and Transatlantic Culture in the 1850s.* Athens: University of Georgia Press, 2005.

Meillassoux, Claude. *The Anthropology of Slavery: The Womb of Iron and Gold.* Chicago: University of Chicago Press, 1991.

Moore, Janie G. "Africanisms among Blacks of the Sea Islands." *Journal of Black Studies* 10, no. 4 (June 1980): 467–80.

Morgan, Philip D. *Slave Counterpoint: Black Culture in the Eighteenth-Century Chesapeake and Lowcountry.* Williamsburg, VA: Omohundro Institute of Early American History and Culture, 1998.

Ogundrian, Akinwumi, and Toyin Falola, eds. *The Archaeology of Atlantic Africa and the African Diaspora.* Bloomington: Indiana University Press, 2007.

Olmsted, Frederick. *A Journey in the Seaboard Slave States: With Remarks on Their Economy.* London: Samson Low, Sons, & Co., 1856.

Orser, Charles. "The Archaeological Analysis of Plantation Society: Replacing Status and Caste with Economics and Power." *American Antiquity* 53, no. 4 (1988): 735–51.

———, ed. *Race and the Archaeology of Identity.* Salt Lake City: University of Utah Press, 2001.

Otto, John S. *Cannons Point Plantation 1794–1860: Living Conditions and Status Patterns in the Old South.* Orlando, FL: Academic Press, 1984.

Parris, Linda E. *A Dutiful Obedient Wife: The Journal of Elizabeth Foote Washington.* Williamsburg, VA: College of William and Mary, 1984.

Phaneuf, Holly. *Herbs Demystified.* New York: Marlow, 2005.

Phillips, Ulritch B. *American Negro Slavery.* Baton Rouge: Louisiana State University Press, 1966.

Pinkard, Susan. *A Revolution in Taste: The Rise of French Cuisine.* Cambridge: Cambridge University Press, 2009.

Purdue, Charles. *Weevils in the Wheat: Interviews with Virginia's Ex-Slaves.* Charlottesville: University of Virginia Press, 1977.

Quimby, Ian M. G., ed. *Material Culture and the Study of American Life.* New York: W. W. Norton, 1978.

Raboteau, Albert J. *Slave Religion: The Invisible Institution in the American South.* Oxford: Oxford University Press, 1980.

Randolph, Mary. *The Virginia Housewife or, Methodical Cook: A Facsimile of an Authentic Early American Cookbook 1824.* New York: Dover, 1993.

Revell, Katherine G. *Research Report with Recommendations for Reinterpreting and Refurnishing Monticello's Kitchen and Related Dependencies.* Jefferson Library, Thomas Jefferson Memorial Foundation, 1996.

Salmon, Emily J., and Edward D. C. Campbell Jr., eds. *The Hornbook of Virginia History.* Richmond: Library of Virginia, 1994.

Schwartz, Philip J. *Twice Condemned: Slaves and the Criminal Laws of Virginia, 1705–1865.* Baton Rouge: Louisiana State University Press, 1988.

Scott, Anne Frior. *The Southern Lady, from Pedestal to Politics, 1830–1930.* Chicago: University of Chicago Press, 1970.

Sharpless, Rebecca. *Cooking in Other Women's Kitchens: Domestic Workers in the South, 1865–1960.* Chapel Hill: University of North Carolina Press, 2013.

Simmons, Amelia. *The First American Cookbook: American Cookery.* Albany, NY: C. R. Webster, 1796.

Singleton, Teresa., ed. *I, Too, Am America: Archaeological Studies of African American Life.* Charlottesville: University of Virginia Press, 1999.

Sobel, Michal. *The World They Made Together: Black and White Values in Eighteenth-Century Virginia.* Princeton, NJ: Princeton University Press, 1987.

South, Stanley A. *Method and Theory in Historical Archaeology.* New York: Academic Press, 1977.

Stamp, Kenneth. *The Peculiar Institution: Slavery in the Ante-Bellum South.* New York: Alfred A. Knopf, 1956.

Tadman, Michael. *Speculators and Slaves: Masters, Traders, and Slaves in the Old South.* Madison: University of Wisconsin Press, 1989.

Taylor, Joe Gray. *Eating, Drinking, and Visiting in the South: An Informal History.* Baton Rouge: Louisiana State University Press, 1982.

Thompson, Robert Farris. *Flash of the Spirit.* New York: Random House, 1983.

Thornton, John Kelly. *Africa and Africans in the Making of the Atlantic World, 1400–1800*. New York: Cambridge University Press, 1998.

Tyree, Marion Cabell, ed. *Housekeeping in Old Virginia*. Louisville, KY: John P. Morton, 1879.

Upton, Dell. "Black and White Landscapes in Eighteenth Century Virginia." In *Material Life in America, 1600–1860*, ed. Robert Blair St. George. Boston: Northeastern University Press, 1988.

———. "Early Vernacular Architecture in Southeastern Virginia." PhD diss., Brown University, 1979.

———. "Vernacular Domestic Architecture in Eighteenth-Century Virginia." *Winterthur Portfolio* 17, no. 2–3 (Summer–Autumn 1982): 95–119.

Vlach, John Michael. *The Afro-American Tradition in Decorative Arts*. Athens: University of Georgia Press, 1990.

———. *Back of the Big House: The Architecture of Plantation Slavery*. Chapel Hill: University of North Carolina Press, 1993.

———. *The Planter's Prospect: Privilege and Slavery in Plantation Paintings*. Chapel Hill: University of North Carolina Press, 2002.

Walsh, Lorena. *From Calibar to Carter's Grove: The History of a Virginia Slave Community*. Charlottesville: University of Virginia Press, 1997.

Washington, Booker T. *Up from Slavery*. Boston: Bedford/St. Martin's, 2003.

Washington, George. *The Diaries of George Washington*. Vol. 4, *1 September 1784–30 June 1786*. Edited by Donald Jackson and Dorothy Twohig. Charlottesville: University Press of Virginia, 1978.

———. *The Papers of George Washington, Colonial Series*. Vol. 8, *24 June 1767–25 December 1771*. Edited by W. W. Abbot and Dorothy Twohig. Charlottesville: University Press of Virginia, 1993.

———. *The Papers of George Washington, Colonial Series*. Vol. 10, *21 March 1774–15 June 1775*. Edited by W. W. Abbot and Dorothy Twohig. Charlottesville: University Press of Virginia, 1995.

———. *The Papers of George Washington, Presidential Series*. Vol. 5, *16 January 1790–30 June 1790*. Edited by Dorothy Twohig, Mark A. Mastromarino, and Jack D. Warren. Charlottesville: University Press of Virginia, 1996.

———. *The Papers of George Washington, Presidential Series*. Vol. 6, *1 July*

1790–30 November 1790. Edited by Mark A. Mastromarino. Charlottesville: University Press of Virginia, 1996.

———. *The Papers of George Washington, Presidential Series*. Vol. 8, *22 March 1791–22 September 1791*. Edited by Mark A. Mastromarino. Charlottesville: University Press of Virginia, 1999.

———. *The Papers of George Washington, Retirement Series*. Vol. 2, *2 January 1798–15 September 1798*. Edited by W. W. Abbot. Charlottesville: University Press of Virginia, 1998.

———. *The Writings of George Washington*. 14 vols. Edited by Worthington Chauncey Ford. New York: G. P. Putnam's Sons, 1889–1893.

Wecter, Dixon. *The Saga of American Society: A Record of Social Aspiration 1607–1937*. New York: Charles Scribner's Sons, 1937.

Weiner, Marli F. *Mistresses and Slaves: Plantation Women in South Carolina, 1830–80*. Urbana: University of Illinois Press, 1998.

Wells, Camille. "The Planter's Prospect: Houses, Outbuildings, and Rural Landscapes in Eighteenth-Century Virginia." *Winterthur Portfolio* 28, no. 1 (Spring 1993): 1–31.

Wenger, Mark R. "The Dining Room in Early Virginia." *Perspectives in Vernacular Architecture* 3 (1989): 149–59.

White, Deborah Gray. *Ar'n't I a Woman? Female Slaves in the Plantation South*. New York: W. W. Norton, 1985.

Wilkie, Laurie A. *The Archaeology of Mothering: An African American Midwives Tale*. New York: Routledge, 2003.

Williams-Forson, Psyche A. *Building Houses out of Chicken Legs: Black Women, Food, and Power*. Chapel Hill: University of North Carolina Press, 2006.

Wright, Gavin. "Slavery and American Agricultural History." *Agricultural History* 77, no. 4 (Autumn 2003): 540–43.

Yentch, Anne Elizabeth. *A Chesapeake Family and Their Slaves*. Cambridge: Cambridge University Press, 1994.

INDEX

Unless otherwise noted, place names are in Virginia.

Alexandria, 94
Alice (slave), 75
Amherst County, 64
Anderson, Patience, 70
Anna (slave), 71
archaeology, 3, 6, 7, 13, 48–49, 71–72, 124, 129, 136–40
architecture, 7, 17–41, 48
Atkinson, Billy, 95
Aunt Jemima, 1–3, 127, 130
Austin (Washington family footman), 79, 82

Bacon, Nathaniel, 92
Bedford County, 94
Berkeley Plantation, 34, 133
Berry Hill Plantation, 34
Bight of Biafra, Africa, 9
Bird, John, 70
Blow, George, 118
Bolling, Mark, 94
Bransford, Daniel, 95
Brown, Liza, 62
Bruce, Eliza, 34
Brunswick, 95

Carrington, Cesar, 94

Carter family, 44–45, 52, 62, 69, 112–13, 116
Charles City County, 17, 21, 24, 40, 62, 69, 90, 112, 116, 133
Charlotte County, 95
Civil War, the, 9, 13, 15
Coleman, Cuffy, 94
Coles, Helen, 113
conjuring, 96, 136–40
Corbin, Mingo, 94
Cosby, Daniel (butler), 58, 68
Crenshaw, Joe, 94
Cumberland County, 94–95
Cunningham, Baily, 70
Custis, Eliza Parke, 88
Custis, George Washington Parke, 82–84
Custis, John Parke, 130

Davey (slave), 92
Dawson, Fanny, 95
Dawson, Renah, 95
Dean, Rueben, 59
Degraffendriedt, Mrs., 117
Delia (Washington family slave), 75, 88
dining rooms, 16, 23, 26, 28, 30, 32, 34, 37, 68, 70–71, 100, 107–8, 119, 121, 133
dinner parties, 11, 16

Index

Dixon Plantation, 71, 139–40
dumbwaiters, 36–37

Emma (cook), 70
enslaved cooks, legacy of, 13, 17, 18, 127–40
Eppes, Richard, 49, 61, 71, 120
Eve (slave), 94
Evey (Washington family slave), 75, 88
Ezell, Roberta, 95

family, 4, 7, 11, 15–17, 29, 40, 63–69, 136–40
Fanny (cook), 89
Fithian, Phillip V., 40, 44, 52, 69, 112–13
Flowerdew Hundred, 8, 48, 136–40
Fossett, Edith (cook), 89
Fossett, Joseph, 91
Fraunces, Samuel, 78
Fredericksburg, 89
furnishings, 38–41, 47–49

George (Eppes family waiter), 71
Giles (slave), 77
Gloucester County, 58
Goochland County, 94
Goode, Fanny, 95
Granger, Ursula (cook), 89
Griffin, Eliza, 95

Hamilton, Sukey (cook), 43, 64
Harriet (cook), 70, 96
Harriet (Eppes family cook), 49
Harrison, Dick, 94

Harrison, Judith, 94
Hemings, James (Jefferson family cook), 88; fame of, 89–90
Hemings, Peter (cook), 89–91
Henrico County, 94
Hercules (Washington family cook), 62, 73–88; escape of, 86; fame of, 82; in Philadelphia, 75–88, 90; as Washington's head chef, 75–77
historic preservation, 17, 18
Holladay family, 59
housing, 4, 11, 15, 19, 40, 45–49
Hudson (slave), 94

Igbo people, 9, 93

Jackson, Susan, 62
James River, 8
Jamestown, 7, 8
Jefferson, Isaac, 89
Jefferson, Thomas, 36, 88–92
Jim Crow era, 134–35
John, Colin, 95
Johnson, Hannah (cook), 70
Jones, Emmanuel (cook), 48, 136–40
Jones, Keziah, 48

Key, Harry, 94
King and Queen County, 71
King James I, 7
Kingsmill Plantation, 8
Kitt, Frederick, 86

landscapes, 11, 13, 17–41

laundresses, 11, 12, 24
laws, 8, 11, 13, 78, 86, 92, 94–98, 134
Lawson, Chastity, 95
Lawson, George, 95
Lear, Tobias, 76–77
Lee family, 27–28
Lewis, Lawrence, 88
liquor, 45, 55–59, 69, 79, 89, 91
Lishy (cook), 59–60
Louisa County, 95
Louis-Philippe, 88
Lucy (Washington family cook), 73
Lucy (Wills family cook), 64
Ludwell, Hannah Harrison, 27
Lunenburg, 94–95

Marshall, William, 89
Mary (slave), 95–97
Mason, Allen, 95
Mason, John, 118
Mason, Reuben, 95
medicine, 9, 92–98, 113
Middlesex, 94
Middleway Plantation, 58
mistresses: Eliza Parke Custis, 88; Mrs. Degraffendriedt, 117; Maria Nelson, 112; Susanna Peachy Poythress, 137; Mary Randolph, 122; Lucy Roy, 95–97; Elizabeth Foote Washington, 109
Mitchell, Delp, 95
Montague, Peter, 94
Monticello, 12, 34, 36, 88–92
Mount Vernon, 34, 73–88

Nathan (cook), 73
Nat Turner rebellion, 16, 36, 138
Nelson, Maria, 112
Nichols, Dow, 95
Nichols, Harry, 95
Nichols, Richard, 95
Nigeria, Africa, 9
Nomini Hall Plantation, 44, 112
Nottoway County, 94–95

Old Betty (cook), 74
Old Doll (cook), 73
Olmsted, Frederick Law, 72, 115
Orange County, 94

passageways, 32–37
Payne, Hampton, 94
Petit, Adrien, 90
Philadelphia, Pennsylvania, 75–88, 90
Phillips, Peter, 94
Piedmont, 10, 12, 22, 64, 88–92
plantation museums, 5, 6, 14, 20, 40–41, 127–40
planters: John Aylett, 61; George Blow, 118; Carter family, 44–45, 52, 62, 69, 112–13, 116; John Parke Custis, 130; Richard Eppes, 49, 61, 71, 120; Thomas Jefferson, 36, 88–92; Lee family, 27–28; Lawrence Lewis, 88; William Marshall, 89; John Mason, 118; Peter Montague, 94; William Plume, 130; Eleanor Pratt, 70; Dr. Augustus Roy, 95–97; Thomas Spragins,

planters *(cont.)*
 64; John Wayles, 90; John V.
 Wilcox, 136; James Wills, 64
Plume, William, 130
poisoning, 14, 16, 73, 92–98
Poplar Forest, 12
Poythress, Susanna Peachy, 137
Pratt, Eleanor, 70
Prince Edward County, 94–95
Prince George County, 48–49,
 62, 136–40
Prosser, Gabriel, 36
punishment/abuse, 11, 15, 62–63

Rachael (cook), 61–62
Randolph (slave), 94
Randolph, Edmund, 78
Randolph, Mary, 122
Read, Mrs., 77, 81–82
recipes, 12, 13, 43, 46, 50–57,
 74–75, 109, 121–25
religion, 138–40
resistance, 16, 36–37, 39, 58, 61–
 63, 73–98, 84–88, 92–98
Reynolds, Dollan, 94
Richmond (Washington family
 slave), 75–78, 85, 88
Richmond, city of, 96–97
Richneck Plantation, 124
Roy, Dr. Augustus, 95–97
Roy, Lucy, 95–97

Sanders, Ursula (cook), 49
Scott, Jessee, 91
service bells, 34
Shirley Plantation, 8, 21, 24, 40,
 116

slaves: Alice, 75; Patience
 Anderson, 70; Anna, 71;
 Billy Atkinson, 95; John
 Bird, 70; Mark Bolling,
 94; Daniel Bransford, 95;
 Cesar Carrington, 94;
 Cuffy Coleman, 94; Mingo
 Corbin, 94; Joe Crenshaw,
 94; Baily Cunningham, 70;
 Davey, 92; Fanny Dawson,
 95; Renah Dawson, 95;
 Delia (Washington family
 slave), 75, 88; Eve, 94; Evey
 (Washington family slave), 75,
 88; Roberta Ezell, 95; Joseph
 Fossett, 91; Giles, 77; Fanny
 Goode, 95; Eliza Griffin, 95;
 Dick Harrison, 94; Judith
 Harrison, 94; Hudson, 94;
 Isaac Jefferson, 89; Colin
 John, 95; Harry Key, 94;
 Chastity Lawson, 95; George
 Lawson, 95; Mary, 95–97;
 Allen Mason, 95; Reuben
 Mason, 95; Delp Mitchell,
 95; Dow Nichols, 95; Harry
 Nichols, 95; Richard Nichols,
 95; Hampton Payne, 94;
 Peter Phillips, 94; Randolph,
 94; Dollan Reynolds, 94;
 Richmond (Washington family
 slave), 75–78, 85, 88; Dick
 Spencer, 95; John Spencer, 95;
 Bob Steinbridge, 95; Ralph
 Strother, 94; Tabby, 95–97;
 Isaac Thornton, 94; Punch
 Wade, 94; Taffy Ware, 94;

Warner, 95–97; Peter Wiley, 94; Shadrach Wilkins, 95–97
slave trade, 35, 37, 121
Sookey (cook), 15, 41
Sparks, Elizabeth (cook), 62
Spencer, Dick, 95
Spencer, John, 95
Spragins, Thomas, 64
Steinbridge, Bob, 95
Stratford Hall Plantation, 27–28
Strawberry Hill Plantation, 59
Strother, David Hunter, 64–65
Strother, Ralph, 94
Stuart, Gilbert, 87
Surry County, 15
Susan (Eppes family cook), 49
Sussex, 95

Tabby (slave), 95–97
theft, 39, 60–61, 85
Thornton, Isaac, 94
Tidewater region, 12, 19, 30
Turner rebellion, 16, 36, 138

Uncle Bob (butler), 58

Vicar, John, 78
Virginia Beach, 95

Wade, Punch, 94
Ware, Taffy, 94
Warner (slave), 95–97
Washington, Booker T., 130
Washington, DC, 91
Washington, Elizabeth Foote, 109
Washington, George, 73–88
Washington, Martha, 73–88
Wayles, John, 90
weddings, 70–71
West African foodways, 3, 4, 11, 14, 56, 92, 114–25
Westmoreland County, 27–28
Westover Plantation, 112
White Sulphur Springs, West Virginia (formerly Virginia), 72
Wilcox, John V., 136
Wilcox Plantation, 136–40
Wiley, Peter, 94
Wilkins, Shadrach, 95–97
Williamsburg, 43, 64, 117, 124, 130
Wills, James, 64
Woodlawn Plantation, 88

York County, 30